Social Awareness Skills for Children

of related interest:

People Skills for Young Adults
Márianna Csóti
ISBN 1 85302 716 2

Understanding and Supporting Children with Emotional and Behavioural Difficulties
Edited by Paul Cooper
ISBN 1 85302 666 2

Helping Children to Build Self-Esteem
A Photocopiable Activities Book
Deborah Plummer
ISBN 1 85302 927 0

Listening to Young People in School, Youth Work and Counselling
Nick Luxmore
ISBN 1 85302 909 2

The Social Skills Game
Yvonne Searle and Isabelle Streng
ISBN 1 85302 336 1

Helping People with a Learning Disability Explore Choice
Eve and Neil Jackson, illustrated by Tim Baker
ISBN 1 85302 694 8

Helping People with a Learning Disability Explore Relationships
Eve and Neil Jackson, illustrated by Tim Baker
ISBN 1 85302 688 3

Asperger's Syndrome
A Guide for Parents and Professionals
Tony Attwood
ISBN 1 85302 577 1

Incorporating Social Goals in the Classroom
A Guide for Teachers and Parents of Children with High-Functioning Autism and Asperger Syndrome
Rebecca A. Moyes
Foreword by Susan J. Moreno
ISBN 1 85302 967 X

Social Awareness Skills for Children

Márianna Csóti

Jessica Kingsley Publishers
London and Philadelphia

The right of the Márianna Csóti to be identified as author of this work has been asserted by her in accordance with the Copyright, Designs and Patents Act 1988.

First published in the United Kingdom in 2001 by
Jessica Kingsley Publishers Ltd,
116 Pentonville Road, London
N1 9JB, England
and
325 Chestnut Street,
Philadelphia, PA 19106, USA.

www.jkp.com

Library of Congress Cataloging in Publication Data
A CIP catalog record for this book is available from the Library of Congress

British Library Cataloguing in Publication Data
A CIP catalogue record for this book is available from the British Library

ISBN 1 84310 003 7

Printed and Bound in Great Britain by
Athenaeum Press, Gateshead, Tyne and Wear

This book is dedicated to my daughter, Emily,
with thanks for all her help

Contents

About the Book

This book is intended for professionals, parents and carers engaged in teaching children communication and social skills, for whatever reason. For example, children with Special Needs (such as Asperger Syndrome, Attention Deficit Disorder and Learning Difficulties) require considerable help in learning how to relate to other people and how to behave positively or appropriately. Other children may not have had socially skilled role models to learn from or they may have failed to pick up on the finer aspects of communication despite having very socially skilled parents or carers.

The book is suitable for children aged about 7 to 16 and comprises a course made up of several small tasks, to be worked through *with* the child, and advice for the professional, parent or carer. Although the tasks in the book have been designed to be worked through on a one-to-one basis, it would be possible to use them with a small group. One advantage of small group work in therapy is that some children who are totally unaware of the social mistakes they make themselves may be able to observe and learn from others' mistakes.

Each task is sufficiently short to allow for frequent breaks within the whole session, so that the child's concentration is only needed in short bursts. Aim to work for up to an hour in each session, but with older children, particularly teenagers, the speed at which the tasks are completed could be greater than that for the younger child, as long as understanding is not compromised. (Parents or carers could work in ten-minute stretches if their child cannot concentrate for longer, since they have the advantage of being 'on hand'.) It is possible to stop at any point throughout the course and continue another time, although it is important to recap at the end of one session and the beginning of the next. Constant revision of ideas is recommended, as children need frequent reinforcement.

The book is practically based with examples to illustrate the ideas discussed, in order to make communication and social skills training familiar territory. This will make it easier to apply it to the child's life. Example answers have been included so that the person leading the session can give the child suggestions or help should she need further explanation of a task. They are not intended to be model answers. Others may be equally or more valid, depending on the special circumstances of a situation.

Introduction

If you think a child's answer to any of the following questions would be 'Yes', then this book is suitable for her.

- Are you shy?
- Are you often ignored?
- Do you feel you are not liked or admired by other people?
- Do you hate having to talk to people you hardly know?
- Is it hard for you to ask your teacher a question or ask her for help?
- Do you dread being singled out from your friends?
- Do you find it hard to make friends (and keep them)?
- Do you have trouble sticking up for yourself?
- Do other children take advantage of you?
- Do people say hurtful things to you (and get away with it)?
- Do you often feel bad about yourself?
- Do you lack confidence?
- Do you prefer to look at the floor than make eye contact?
- Do you stoop or slouch, especially when you feel awkward about something?
- Do you bully other children?
- Do you lash out when you are angry?
- Do you throw tantrums?
- Are you bullied?
- Has any adult made you do something you feel uncomfortable about?
- Do you sometimes not know how to behave in certain situations?

- Do you lack tact?
- Do you interrupt other people's conversations at inappropriate moments?
- Are you unaware of when you bore people?
- Do you only have one-sided conversations, with you always talking or you always listening to someone else?
- Do you feel isolated or rejected?

This book comprises a course in social awareness skills which includes communication and social skills, the skills needed to help children overcome the above problems. Communication skills are about being able to communicate, without misunderstandings on either side, and social skills are about being sensitive to others and respecting them in the way that one relates to them. Communication and social skills are essential aspects of becoming socially aware and socially skilled.

Communication skills

To be a good communicator, a child needs to be able to give the right messages, so that she is clearly understood. This involves speaking distinctly, understanding body language, showing her feelings in an appropriate way and being able to explain herself. She also needs to be skilled at reading other people's messages and interpreting them. (Do they actually mean that, or, because they laughed, am I being teased?)

Part of being socially skilled is having good communication skills. A child cannot be socially skilled if people misunderstand her and take offence. She cannot make friends if she is unable to chat to them or relate to them on their level and she cannot successfully relate to the adults in her life if she is too shy or awkward to talk to them or ask them for help. Communication skills also help protect her in awkward situations.

Social skills

Social skills are to do not only with a child being polite to others but also with explaining her needs in such a way that others can take her seriously and respect her opinions. They are to do with respecting others – that means dealing with them without bullying them or saying things deliberately to hurt; respecting other religions, cultures and other races. And they are to do with respecting herself – showing others that she is worth a lot to herself.

It is also important for a child to show sensitivity to others and understanding of others' points of view and to be able to negotiate a middle road in times of conflict.

Why do we need to teach communication and social skills?

The acquisition of communication and social skills is usually left entirely to chance, apart from a few obvious instructions to a child (for example, telling her to say 'Please', 'Thank you' and 'Thank you for having me'). Some children are lucky: they have socially skilled parents or carers who are good communicators *and* have had the privilege to observe them in social situations, so learning to copy, adapt and develop what they see. Others are not so lucky; reasons for this may be:

- Their parents or carers may have lacked skilful communication and social skills and they pass that lack on to their own children.

- Their parents or carers may be socially skilled but the children fail to observe this behaviour and so it is not accessible to them.

- Their parents or carers may feel awkward when meeting others and so their children may not have had the opportunity to observe positive social behaviour.

- The children may have particular problems that have meant they have not developed appropriate social skills.

Instead of leaving it to chance whether a child picks up on these essential life-skills, it is better to teach them.

Why does a child need to learn communication and social skills?

Children who do not develop good communication and social skills may have a string of failing or failed relationships, without ever knowing why. This could leave them hurt and confused, making them feel bad about themselves. This lowers their self-esteem and dents their confidence, making it even more likely that they will be unsuccessful in their relationships in the future.

To be able to exercise good social skills and not be afraid of communicating their thoughts and feelings, children need to have confidence and a high self-esteem. Chapters 2 and 3 are concerned with strengthening these shortcomings.

Communication and social skills training is not merely about how to behave when meeting people from outside the family – it is training for a clearer and more honest form of communication that pervades every aspect of life, from within the home to all situations outside the home. It also shows one how to listen and support others, how to read people's body language and pick up on the many cues they give to convey certain messages: many problems arise when these are not recognised or are misinterpreted.

In addition to communication and social skills, social awareness skills include knowledge and understanding of social expectations in certain places and within certain situations, and social safety. Social awareness skills allow the child to grow and understand human nature more thoroughly.

The aim of the book

The aim of the book is to show you how to help a child:

- boost her self-esteem
- respect herself
- respect other people
- respect differences between people
- make friends and keep them
- understand the different roles people have in different situations
- understand the social rules that need to be followed in certain places and in certain situations
- be a good communicator
- show her feelings
- control her anger
- behave assertively
- have the confidence to stand up for herself
- not be embarrassed or ashamed to ask for help when she needs it
- reduce negative behaviour towards others and herself
- negotiate
- predict the consequences of her actions
- receive compliments gracefully and give meaningful compliments to others
- be non-judgemental
- be a good listener

- empathise with other people.

Whatever the reason for underdeveloped communication and social skills, this book will help the child understand how to behave positively towards others without compromising culture, beliefs, traditions and values.

Author's note

- To avoid the continual use of he/she in this book, 'she' has been used to encompass both sexes.

- To avoid the continual use of parent/carer in this book, the word parent has been used to mean any adult who is in the position of being the main carer for the child. This person may be her natural birth parent, her adoptive or foster parent, an adult who looks after children in care or another relative such as a grandparent. When the word parents is used, this may mean either a couple or one person who has sole responsibility for the child.

- When a child is referred to as 'playing with' another, swap this expression for 'socialising with' for a teenager.

- The course begins in Chapter 2.

- You will need an A4 ring binder file and plenty of A4 paper on which to write the child's responses to the exercises. (If she is older, she may be able to write the responses herself although she may have difficulty summarising the ideas.) If all the pages are kept together in a file, she can easily remind herself of all the things that were talked about between you at any time in the future. It will give her something special to keep. The ideas addressed are valid for people of any age – she may wish to use them well into adulthood.

- Some pages are photocopiable for professionals to use with parents. These pages are denoted by the symbol [✓].

- For older and more able children, some chapters may be completed in one session an hour long. However, the speed at which you complete the chapter may vary depending on the ability of the child with whom you are working and on how significant the chapter is for that child. The timing is unimportant. For example, a child who is a beginner at understanding about body language may need to spend much more time on Chapters 6 and 7. You can stop and start again later at any point in the book (in order). However, it is important that when you reach the end of a chapter you summarise, with the child's help, what she has learnt from that section and what things need to be remembered and why.

- Some tasks may be omitted altogether if they are inappropriate for the child's age or ability. Some concepts are harder to understand (such as 'Roles' in Chapter 4), but have been included to challenge older children and to make the course complete. The child can return to the course at a later stage in her life and benefit from a more in-depth approach; this allows the course to grow with the child.

- A child needs to experience unconditional regard: to know that despite whatever failings she or you feel she has, you respect her. (In the case of parents helping their child, add unconditional love to unconditional regard.) This is vital to having a confident child with a high self-esteem.

Chapter 1

Children with Special Needs;
Professional and Parental Help

Children who have poor social skills are often lonely, have few friends and suffer social rejection and isolation. Later in life, they may have difficulty finding and keeping employment. Children who are socially isolated and rejected are at greater risk of emotional disorders (such as depression and panic attacks) and behavioural disorders (such as anti-social behaviour and delinquency).

Children with Special Needs

Children with Special Needs are at still higher risk of emotional and behavioural disorders than those who have poor social skills alone. Often, the impaired cognitive development (knowing about and perceiving the world around them) and impaired emotional and social development from which they suffer can lead to social and academic failure, increasing the likelihood of their becoming anti-social and delinquent.

Other factors increase the likelihood of anti-social behaviour. For example, some children with Attention Deficit (Hyperactive) Disorder may be predisposed towards aggression and, unfortunately, may be less responsive to punishments or lack understanding of the consequences of what they have done. This, in turn, can lead to dislike of school and of those in authority, and a rejection of the values held by them.

It is important to help all children with poor social skills, and most particularly those with Special Needs, at as early an age as possible to prevent the downward spiral of social rejection and failure leading to anti-social behaviour and emotional problems later in life.

Some children may never achieve very socially skilled behaviour but with help, they may achieve a level of social competence that will enable them to perform positively in society. With help they may fulfil their basic needs of friendship, be socially included and employable and will have learnt what behaviour is unacceptable and understand the reasons why.

Pervasive Development Disorder

Autism and Asperger Syndrome (plus other related disorders) come under the broad heading of Pervasive Development Disorder (a neurological disorder that affects brain function). It is characterised by impairment in several areas of development (one on its own is insufficient for such a diagnosis to be made), all children showing deficits in communication and social skills, but differing in severity. Both autistic and Asperger children may have differing severity of symptoms at different stages of their lives and their typical behaviours may change or improve over time.

AUTISM

Autism is a spectrum disorder, meaning that there is a full range of abilities and severity of problems: sufferers can have any combination of a number of symptoms to any degree. Sufferers of autism may have other disorders that also affect brain function such as epilepsy, mental retardation or genetic disorders. Autism is apparent before the age of 30 months.

Autistic children become increasingly unresponsive to parents' affection and resist being cuddled. They remain aloof from people and fail to form relationships, preferring to play alone and finding it hard or impossible to play co-operatively with other children. They are often indifferent to social conventions and lack the ability to understand other people's feelings.

Autistic children have great difficulties with learning language and find it hard to communicate with others (both verbally and non-verbally); they lack the ability to understand or copy gestures. Speech, when acquired, is robot-like and monotonal, without the variation of higher and lower pitch. The children can be extremely hyperactive or passive and behave impulsively. They may have temper tantrums or cry for no apparent reason. Their symptoms and abilities can vary from day to day.

Some children may show aggression or be self-injurious and they often have repeated body movements such as rocking or hand flapping and dislike changes in routine, to the extent that they resist learning new skills as they like things to remain the same. Some children may also have sensitivity in the five senses of touch, sight, hearing, taste and smell.

Children with autism show uneven skill development (unlike those who are mentally retarded, where the development of all skills is at a similar level): they may have highly developed skills in areas, for example, other than language such as in music and drawing or in memorising facts. Autism is about three to four times more common in boys than girls.

ASPERGER SYNDROME

Asperger Syndrome is part of the autism spectrum but it is characterised by greater language abilities. Asperger children have language skills at or slightly below the average, whereas children diagnosed with autism usually have extreme difficulty in learning language and most never develop normal speech. Asperger children also often have average or above average intelligence. Usually, delays in social, communicative and cognitive development are noted within the first 12 months.

Children with Asperger Syndrome often interrupt conversations at inappropriate moments to talk about some topic wholly unrelated to that currently under discussion. They like to dominate conversations, usually talking about something with which they are obsessed, and do not worry about whether the other person is interested in what they have to say. Such conversations are not 'social' as they are one-sided, focusing on one person's interests alone with total disregard for the other's needs and without trying to make the experience rewarding.

Also, children with Asperger Syndrome are usually unable to read facial expressions or pick up on body language or social cues. They need to be taught to look for these and how to interpret what they see. They may also have difficulty keeping eye contact with someone they are talking to, which is an essential part of communicating person to person. Like autistic children, they like routine and may fix on a particular item or idea. Far more boys than girls are diagnosed with Asperger Syndrome.

Attention Deficit (Hyperactive) Disorder

Attention Deficit Disorder is a syndrome which is usually characterised by poor attention span, impulsivity and hyperactivity (but not in all cases). Affected children can suffer from other conditions such as Learning Difficulties, have delayed speech development and have Obsessive Compulsive Disorders.

Children with Attention Deficit (Hyperactive) Disorder are easily distracted and are inattentive (they may make careless mistakes or may not pay close attention to detail, or may be forgetful of what needs to be done). They often have difficulty following instructions, frequently not listening to what is being said. They may have difficulty organising tasks, disliking tasks that require sustained effort and losing the things they need to complete them.

Those that are hyperactive have difficulty in remaining seated or in performing an activity quietly, talking excessively. They often fidget with their hands or feet or in their seat.

They also have a tendency to be impulsive: not considering the consequences of their actions, being tactless or being unable to wait their turn at games or in speech, often blurting out an answer to a question given to another child and frequently interrupting, appearing bossy, insensitive and rude.

Many children with Attention Deficit (Hyperactive) Disorder have difficulty following social rules and understanding what is expected in different social situations and so must be taught what to do when.

In addition to behavioural problems, some children with Attention Deficit (Hyperactive) Disorder suffer from anxiety disorders and many more from depression. About three times as many boys as girls are diagnosed with this condition and, for some, the condition improves with age.

Learning Difficulties

Generally, children with Learning Difficulties have a measure of overlap with some of the above problems. Many children with Learning Difficulties (and/or the above problems) are unable to change their behaviour in response to changing demands, and so their behaviour may often seem inappropriate for a particular situation. They may be unable to control their emotions, the result being outbursts, temper tantrums, overreaction, impatience and limited self-awareness. The lack of emotional control increases the risk of behavourial problems, anxiety and depression.

Children who behave awkwardly and inappropriately in social situations and who are socially imperceptive (not picking up on body language cues or messages given by other people by fine adjustment of behaviour) may feel isolated and uninvolved with their peers and even rejected. They may be ignored or subjected to ridicule, harassment or bullying. This can put children off going to school, as the way they feel about school may depend on their social success – or lack of it.

School phobia

School phobia is not a true phobia but because such intense fear centres around the school environment, causing extreme physical symptoms, it is so conveniently called. Some professionals prefer to call it school refusal.

School phobia can be considered to be of two types. Children with school phobia up to age 8 usually suffer from separation anxiety. (This is frequently accompanied by agoraphobia, where the child is unable to travel on public transport, fearing being ill and developing panic attacks.) The child's reluctance to go to school centres around her lack of confidence and independence because of feelings of insecurity triggered by many possible causes. Examples include feeling threatened by having a new sibling in the family, a parent becoming very ill and having a long break from school themselves through illness or because of a summer holiday. Sometimes the trigger is due to marital problems and a break up of marriage. Most school phobia starts in the first term of the year around September and October.

Children over age 8 more frequently suffer a form of school phobia that is really social phobia or performance anxiety. Things like answering in class, having to read aloud in front of others, being picked last for games and being physically uncoordinated can cause immense stress for children. Teasing and criticism from peers and/or teachers can make a child dread evaluation from anyone in the school environment.

Even if your child has overcome a bout of school phobia, he or she is more prone to suffering it again in the future. For example, a seven-year-old may have recovered from a severe case of school phobia. But she is at greater risk than others of having school phobia when she starts secondary school, when there are new pressures to contend with.

A school phobic child has Special Needs. For a time in her life, the child is made unwell by going to school. Some children suffer so badly that they are either removed from school by their parents to be educated at home or they have to be taught in a Special Unit where the environment is cosier and less threatening than the school environment. Or they may spend years of misery with unresolved anxieties causing other psychological disorders later in life such as depression and panic disorder (where the sufferer has unexpected panic attacks with no apparent trigger). Teenagers who are suffering from constant anxieties may turn to drug, alcohol or solvent abuse to try to numb the feelings they have for some respite.

Teaching social awareness skills to a child can aid her recovery from school phobia and, particularly for the social phobic children, it can help prevent a recurrence later in life. These skills help the child become more confident and more able to manage relationships so that they are positive and non-destructive. They can also help protect a child from bullying, which is another reason why children can refuse to go to school.

Friendships form an important part of a child's life. It is vital that all children have every chance of making a success of these relationships. We practise on our friends and use the knowledge of our successes and mistakes to develop more meaningful relationships as we get older. In our adult life, we need to have satisfying and rewarding friendships to give us support, to guard against depression, to aid getting a job and keeping it, and to relate successfully to many different people in all areas of life. For those children who have a lower starting point than the majority, it is essential that they be taught these skills, so often taken for granted by others, to even the balance and ensure their happiness and social success.

Suggestions for teachers to help Special Needs and socially incompetent children become socially integrated and to raise their self-esteem

This section has been included because children spend a large proportion of their time in school, under the care of teachers who have a valuable input to the child's life.

A child's perception of school vastly depends on her social success within that school environment. A popular child will probably enjoy school, whereas someone who has few friends is less likely to. Academic success alone does not make a child happy and, with the unpopular child, may lead to bullying – the child may be called a 'swot' or be shunned through others' jealousy.

Every child would like to have good friends who seek her company and include her in their games and private chats. Being liked and respected by peers is essential to a child's self-esteem and, if these qualities are absent, she will feel rejected and isolated.

Children who have Learning Difficulties experience academic failure and may be considered to have a low status within the class by their peers and, perhaps, their teachers. They may be perceived as less important or worthy of their peers' and teachers' attention. Long-term school failure demoralises children, destroys self-esteem, and undermines confidence, distancing the child from her teachers, parents and school, and the values they promote. Children can lose hope and cease to believe that their efforts make a difference in their achievements. Also, academic failure can cause stress, which itself impedes learning. Schools that are highly evaluative and authoritarian further increase stress for the child and make her feel more helpless than ever.

Since a child's view of herself is largely dependent on how others behave towards her, any negative messages that she gets will directly affect her self-esteem. As she spends so much time in school and most, if not all, her friends are likely to attend the same institution, it is vital she finds school attendance a positive experience.

Once a child recognises her low status she may be reluctant to interact with others, fearing more social failure, and this will make her feel more rejected and isolated than before. If this downward spiral were to continue, the low-status child might become a low-status adult, having few or no friends, feeling very unworthy and unable effectively to communicate socially at a level sufficient for the work environment.

Protection and nurture of Special Needs and socially incompetent children in school

In school, the teacher can help to reverse the negative effect of social and academic failure and can try to help the child find social and academic success. The following are some suggestions of how to protect and nurture these children.

- Praise all the children within the class whenever possible so that the child is taught in a positive and rewarding environment.

- Help the child perform to a basic social level by giving specific instructions. For example, 'If someone talks to you, stop what you are doing. Look the person in the face and listen to what he has to say. When he has finished speaking you can reply.'

- Observe the child to discover any hidden talents or interests, such as being good at drawing or being involved in an interesting hobby. Then show her work to the rest of the class or ask her to talk about her hobby. In publicly praising a child, you raise her status within the whole class.

- Remind the child of her talents and what she is good at so that she sees herself as a person able to do certain things rather than as someone who fails at everything. It is important for the child to have a positive self-image.

- If the child has particular talents such as in music or athletics, use these lessons to lavish the praise that is absent elsewhere.

- Closely supervise the child so that you can keep her on track when she starts to deviate from expectations rather than after the event when the child has shown herself to have 'failed'. Encourage and nurture rather than being critical and angry.

- Reward acceptable behaviour to reduce disruptive or aggressive behaviour.

- Keep reminding the child what you expect and be consistent.

- Keep instructions brief and be prepared to repeat them.

- Try to introduce situations where the child can succeed rather than fail. If you know a particular task is beyond the child, break it up into more manageable steps so that the child can be rewarded at each small stage rather than feel swamped by a huge task she thinks is insurmountable.

- Give warning before the lesson is to end so that the child does not feel cheated by not having the information. She can then apply herself if her concentration has drifted. ('Fifteen minutes left', 'Ten minutes', etc.)

- If the child has a diagnosed problem, explain it to the others in the class so that they become more understanding and tolerant. This may help the child be socially accepted, as the other children see the problem as a recognised medical condition. (Ask the child's permission first and explain why you think it may help.)

- Do not always allow the know-alls to answer questions you put to the class. Wait to see who else may put up their hand. If a child were to put up her hand for the very first time, ask her to answer. If the answer is incorrect, don't just say 'No' and go on to the next child. Explain to the whole class why the answer might have been feasible, or why it is a common mistake to make, to protect the child from giggles and put-downs from her peers. This will help raise her self-esteem and show her that you valued her contribution. If the answer is correct, openly praise the child in front of her peers to encourage the class to see the child in a better light and boost her self-esteem.

- If you think there is a good chance a child may know an answer you have put to the class but is too afraid to put up her hand, gently ask her the question. Be ready to withdraw your attention if she cannot give an answer, so that she is not humiliated. If she does give an answer, but it is incorrect and a common mistake to make, ask the rest of the class if they agree with her before telling them whether she is right. Then, if half the class have made the same mistake, she might not feel so alone. If the answer is correct, lavish praise on her.

- When pupils need to work in pairs, you could pair off the less able and less socially skilled children with the more able and more socially skilled, so that they are helped and have more opportunity to pick up communication skills from someone more socially confident.

- Avoid asking children to pick their own teams or groups if it is obvious that some will be rejected. This avoids a child always being the last, or nearly last, to be picked.

- Another reason to pair off children or form them into groups yourself is to achieve well-balanced teams with a good mix of abilities within each.

- If miscreant children are grouped together for punishment there may be group approval of deviant behaviour and a greater chance of further anti-social behaviour due to social inclusion in this small group. It is a good idea to separate deviant children in class too, so that they do not strongly identify with one another.

- Provide opportunities for the child to bond with you, the teacher, and with other socially competent children so that she identifies with people who are socially skilled and will therefore be more likely to adopt socially acceptable behaviour. This also reduces the risk of the child bonding with deviant children and adopting deviant behaviour.

- Recognise all positive behaviour in order to provide an incentive for the child to continue with that behaviour and increase the bonding already in progress.

- Group activities help children develop relationships within the group and adopt the group's prosocial (positive social) behaviour.

- Give the child responsibilities such as handing out or collecting textbooks, so that she has a role to play while interacting with her peers. Use every opportunity to get her in a role that makes her peers dependent on her, such as being in charge of handing out materials.

- Ask the child to take messages to other teachers, or to the school secretary, to give her practice in communicating with people in authority.

- Always show respect for the child and demand that her peers do likewise. If you see or hear bullying behaviour, stop it immediately and explain to all concerned that such behaviour is unacceptable. Offer an alternative for the person to do or say. ('Instead of hitting out because someone accidentally tripped you up, stop them and explain what they have done to you.')

- When giving instructions to the class, ensure that you have all their attention first. ('I want you to stop what you're doing and listen. I need to see you all looking at me so that I know I have your attention. Good...') A way of ensuring that they do listen attentively is regularly to ask a member of the class to repeat your instruction to the others. This gives an opportunity for those that suffer from inattentiveness to hear the instruction a second time without you making it obvious – you would be perceived as merely checking that another child has been listening. From time to time, ask the inattentive child to repeat the instruction, when you are sure she was listening and would have a good chance of succeeding, to make her feel important and experience a small success. This will help children get used to addressing the whole class and will aid social confidence.

- Never make a joke at the expense of a child. She will feel humiliated and the joke may well be continued in the playground and get out of hand.

- Always be warm and enthusiastic about the lesson (or pretend to be) and show the children you enjoy being with them by smiling at them, walking round the class and checking that they understand what to do and praising them for their progress. Try to value each individual in some way.

- Encourage the children to ask for help when needed. However, try to lead them into answering the question for themselves where possible so that they experience the pride of having worked it out.

- One-to-one support, particularly with reading skills, can greatly improve a child's performance and make other work more accessible.

SUMMARY

Although schools cannot change underlying medical problems that affect children's cognitive, social and emotional performance, they can help prevent impairments from causing academic and social failure.

Academic failure can be reduced, or prevented, by teachers giving tasks appropriate to the child's level, broken up into accessible pieces. Recognition of the child's particular talents helps boost the child's self-esteem so that she does not perceive herself as failing.

Social failure can be prevented by providing appropriate support and encouragement, concentrating on the social success of the individual within the classroom by promoting bonding with the child's peers and the teacher. Other practices that promote the transfer of prosocial behaviour and beliefs to children are the creation of a consistent system of expectations, reinforcement and recognition to shape the child's behaviour.

Suggested teacher expectations

It is good practice to have a clear idea in your own mind of what you expect from your pupils. It is vital to impart this to all the children in your care so that they know what is expected of them. If all the social rules of the class are clear to all pupils, eventually they should adopt them. The following are some examples of class social rules.

- No one is to talk when you are addressing the whole class.

- When you ask the children to stop what they are doing and listen, you expect them to show respect and do as they have been asked.

- No one should interrupt a child answering a question. Nor should anyone answer the question for that child. They should allow the child time to think about it. If another child wishes to answer instead, she must put up her hand and wait to be invited to answer.

- No one should call out her answer without being invited to, unless it is a more casual discussion-type lesson and you have explained the change of expectation.

- When the children are asked to work as a team, they must fairly share out the tasks and apparatus/materials and treat each member equally and with respect. They should listen to the ideas the others in the team have and consider them. If they reject the ideas, they should be able to explain to the person why.

- There must be no pushing, shoving or snatching. No shouting or screaming.

- When a child speaks to you, or others, she must look you, or others, in the eye.

- When a child enters the class late, she must apologise to you and give an explanation.

- If a child comes in when the door is shut, she must close it again afterwards.

- The children should praise their fellow classmates when they have done something of note or something they have found hard to achieve.

Of course, it would be inappropriate to rattle off all of the above in one go: each point could be introduced when appropriate. Once it has been introduced, the class should be reminded whenever necessary.

Parental help

If the child's social skills are very poor, with the help of the head of pastoral care, you could talk to the child's parents and give them a list of things to work on to help their child. They needn't tackle the whole list in one go – you could work out a plan of stages so that the subsequent stage is not attempted until the child has succeeded at the first. If this were to be done, it would be important to prioritise the skills with the most essential first.

Involving the child's parents also helps bond the teacher to the child's family and with teacher, parents and child working towards a common goal, it is more likely that the child will adopt socially acceptable behaviour.

How Parents Can Help Raise Their Child's Self-Esteem

Photocopiable for professional use within the institution that bought the book, to use to help parents raise their child's self-esteem. These sheets complement the material in Chapter 2.

Any adult closely connected with a child is responsible for that child's positive self-image. If your child thinks badly of herself, consider the following:

- How do you speak to her? (Do you talk down to her, or speak unnecessarily harshly?)

- What do you say when you get angry with her? (Do you call her stupid? Are you sarcastic? – 'Oh, that was clever!')

- Do you blame her for things that were not her fault? ('Now look what you made me do…')

- Are you impatient with her much of the time?

- Do you nag her for being late? (It is your responsibility to ensure a young child has plenty of time to get ready, for example, for school or for an appointment. If you are running late, don't blame her unless she is deliberately obstructive.)

- Do you take things out on her because she is an easy target? (This is like bullying.)

- Do you put her down? ('Trust you to do something like that' – this is a form of bullying, making her feel bad about herself.)

- Is your child's unquestioning obedience more important to you than the reasons why she does the things she does? Do you ever ask why she's done something before deciding whether she should be punished? It is hard for young children to give a clear picture of events and to stand up for themselves. They often don't have the necessary communication skills. They are more likely to stomp around than explain why they think you've been unjust, so it is up to you to try to get your child to explain her behaviour.

✓

- Do you ignore your child's emotional needs? (Are you too busy to spend time with her? Do you notice when she's sad or unhappy? Do you expect her to keep out of your way for long periods? Do you take the time to listen to her when she wants to tell you something?)

- Do you get angry with her for little reason or with no warning? Do you explain that you only said what you did because you were tired or had a bad day? Do you ever ask her forgiveness?

- Do you recognise your child's needs? Do you notice when she's bored or fed up? Ill or tired? Do you anticipate her needs before they become vital? If so, this can smooth a rocky path between you. It is better to react before a crisis develops, where possible.

- Do you take what your child says seriously? If she doesn't think you take any notice of her, it will lower her self-esteem.

- Are you affectionate with your child? Children need unconditional love. They need to know that whatever they do or don't do, you will always love them. They need to be told and shown they are loved.

- Do you worry your child with silly rules? ('If you do that, you might…' or, 'Don't do that, it's not clean, you might catch something' – when it's fairly harmless – or, 'Don't eat that, it'll make you fat' – when your child is far from fat!)

- Do you use out of date rules that were used with you by your parents? (For example, 'You can't possibly go out dressed like that!' – when it's what she's chosen to wear because she likes it and it makes her feel good. Only intervene if it's obvious she's too old to be 'dressing up' or if it's dirty or has holes in and she's young enough for it to be your responsibility that she looks well cared for.) Question the validity of your parents' 'rules' and, if you no longer agree with them, don't repeat them.

- Do you try to make amends? Try to eradicate all the unfair comments you make to her – or apologise the next time you say them and explain why you have been horrible. ('I'm sorry. I've had a bad day and don't feel well.') Excusing yourself in this way must also mean that you listen to her when she's had a bad day and lower your expectations of her behaviour at that time.

Boost your child's self-esteem

The above suggestions help remove some of the things that damage a child's self-esteem. The next advice works for positively improving it:

- If your child has a diagnosed condition, find out as much as you can about it and how best to support her. Explain to your child why she has the difficulties that she has and that it isn't her fault. Encourage her to let you both work as a team to make things easier for her. It is important not to alienate your child: she has a special problem and will need special attention.

- Tell your child that you love her and always will, no matter what she does or doesn't do.

- Tell your child that you like her for her wonderful qualities such as: her cheerfulness, her cheeky ways, her sense of fun, her sympathy for when you feel unwell…

- Tell your child that you are proud of her for being: kind and gentle with babies and toddlers when they pull her hair and hit her with their toys; for getting such a lovely report – it's so nice to read such lovely things about her. Tell her you're proud of her when she does her best and that's all you want.

- Smile at her.

- Share your things with her, including memories and funny moments.

- Have fun together.

- Laugh with her at jokes you can share. Be silly together.

- Spend time with her.

- Listen to what she has to say.

- Play games with her – both physical and non-physical.

- Invite friends for her to socialise with.

- Give her responsibilities within her ability to make her feel useful and needed.

- Compliment her on her appearance or on something she's done well (such as tidying her room or scoring a goal).

Give your child encouragement

You can encourage your child by:

- being sympathetic when she finds something hard or is worried about something

- reassuring her that she has coped in the past

- giving her hugs and kisses

- praising her and applauding her when she has succeeded at something.

All these things help her to:

- increase her confidence

- have happy, outgoing relationships

- be more likely to try to achieve (and succeed) as she knows she has your support

- be more positive about approaching things that are hard

- be less likely to give up

- cope with failure and try a second time

- approach you when she is in trouble and needs help.

Increase your child's self-respect

You increase your child's self-respect by treating her with respect. This means doing the following:

- Accepting that there are some foods she does not like and trying to substitute them with other foods giving similar nutrients.

✓

- Listening to what she has to say and responding to her comments seriously without laughing at her or putting her down.

- Allowing her to help and praising her for it.

- Ignoring small mistakes and smoothing over catastrophes.

- Spending time listening about her day or something she wants to tell you.

- Giving plenty of affection.

- Doing a task together and learning together. You are then treating her as an equal and she will appreciate it.

- Recognising when she has improved or moved forwards in some way, praising her for the progress she's made.

- Telling others about her achievements so she can bask in their praise too. (She could 'phone her grandmother to tell her about it or, if she is very young, you could tell her teacher so that he or she can tell the class).

- Celebrating privately for achievements others may not understand (for example, conquering a habit of biting nails or of picking her nose in public).

- Using your child's mistakes positively. Try to find out why the things happened and then work at ways to prevent them happening in the future. Discuss them fully and openly with your child so that you give her responsibility, and help her develop control over her own actions.

Show you care for your child's wellbeing

Your child will feel nurtured and loved if you show you care about the following.

- The diet she gets. Explain how important a balanced diet is and how she needs to eat plenty of fresh fruit and vegetables as well as bread, pasta, rice and potatoes. Limit the sweets and sugary drinks. Her body is too precious to overload it with unhealthy foodstuffs.

- Her clothes. She needs to wear clean clothes that are reasonably co-ordinated and fit her. Trousers that rise above her ankles when they are not supposed to and tops that expose rather much of her wrists will make her feel embarrassed if her friends all have well-fitting clothes. (This does not mean you must go out and buy the latest designer wear or special sports gear. Always stay within your budget. Jumble sales and car boot sales often have a good selection of clothes. There are also nearly new shops, and adverts in the local paper sometimes identify sellers of clothes. There are sales and discount shops too.)

- Her hair. Your child will need to have her hair cut regularly – by you, a friend or a professional – to make it look neat. It also needs to be washed regularly and combed before she goes out in the morning. If she is at risk from catching head lice, it's a good idea to comb it at night too, in case she has picked up lice during the day. (This damages the lice so that they are unable to lay eggs.)

- How she does in school. Help her with anything she finds hard.

- If someone takes advantage of her or bullies her. Be angry on her behalf and, if possible, talk to the person concerned or his parents or your child's teacher.

Allow your child responsibility over her wellbeing

A child will feel more in control of her life if you give her as much responsibility as you can in looking after herself. It will also teach her independence and give her confidence to do things alone.

- Let your child choose how she wants her hair cut (short, long, a bob, a crew cut) and styled (plaits, pigtails, pony-tail, loose) – as long as it complies with school rules. If, however, your child's fringe is in her eyes it is reasonable for you to say she must either have it cut or fix it back in some way.

- Let your child choose what she wants to wear each day, unless she has a school uniform and there is no choice. But even then, she may choose on the weekends and in the holidays.

- If you are buying your child new clothes, take her with you so that she can choose for herself. She may appreciate them more if she has a hand in the decision.

- As soon as your child is able, give her extra responsibility. When she can, let her dress herself, bath herself, wash her own hair, brush her own teeth (although you may feel more comfortable about doing this yourself for a little longer, to ensure your child has healthy teeth).

- Give her a choice of which vegetables or fruit she is to eat.

- If she cuts herself, it is up to her to clean the wound and put antiseptic cream on – or to ask you to do it for her.

- If someone bullies her, she must come and tell you.

- She must let you know where she is and with whom, at all times. She must learn the rules to keep herself safe. (See Chapter 12, 'Task: Parents: Personal Safety Rules'.)

- If she has a problem, tell her she must *make* you listen, and not allow you to put her off if you're busy. She must keep trying. (See the suggested role-play in Chapter 8, 'Task: Protecting Yourself'.)

Rewarding your child

It is very important for your child to feel good about herself the majority of the time. She will respond more to praise than harsh judgements (although they may well be needed at times). Try to reinforce all your child's positive behaviour with praise and rewards. For example, if she achieves something big, think of an appropriate way to reward your child.

Using the book

Where suggested answers or responses are given, they should be used by the professional or parent to prompt the child – or to give her, or the professional/parent, ideas. The child's file should not become an exact replica of the author's suggested responses (although if the suggestions are the most appropriate for that particular child, they may be used). In many cases, the child's life will yield pertinent examples that she can 'own' and relate to and these will be far more meaningful than any thrust upon her that are outside her personal experience. (Other suggestions from the book, if deemed suitable, can be added at a later stage, when they become appropriate to use.)

The language used in the book is aimed at the professional and parent. Occasionally, when the responses have been given in the child's 'voice', the author has avoided using harder words. However, the majority of suggestions have been made in the professional's or parent's 'voice' (adult 'voice') and these should not be replicated in the child's file as they stand – unless the child has the language to cope with it. The language here has not been simplified, because the author felt it was the most appropriate way to impart a precise meaning to the professional or parent.

Many instructions and helpful suggestions that are given in the adult 'voice' are to help the professional or parent explain and give instructions to the child without having to worry about the sense of the sentence. Many can be used as they stand to communicate the task but they have been written with the intention of explaining the ideas to the adult who can then impart them to the child, not necessarily reading them word for word out loud. Children who have language difficulties may need a very simplified version of the explanations.

Some headings are to be copied into the child's file. The suggested responses to these are written in the child's 'voice' so that the professional or parent need not change the sense of the sentence when writing these, or simplified answers, in the child's file (after they have been independently thought of by, or discussed with, the child).

Parental use

Whatever your child's age, regularly put aside time to work with her. Should there be a break of several days, or even weeks, between sessions, that is no problem at all. Your child will need time to think about the ideas in her own time and in her own way – to assimilate what has been discussed – and she may even get the opportunity to put what she has learnt into practice to consolidate the course. You can help her do this by pointing out forthcoming situations she could use as real-life practice and discussing possible positive behaviour or comments she could employ.

For a child who has particular difficulty with any area of the communication/social skills programme, allow plenty of time for her to adapt to the new expected behaviour before moving on to something equally challenging. Small steps taken slowly are more likely to result in permanent changes in your child's behaviour than large steps rushed and easily forgotten about.

Some of the tasks should be fun, such as the role-play exercises. Enjoy this time spent with your child and remember that you are investing far more than time and energy. You are contributing to your child's psychological and social wellbeing, enabling her to function more confidently as a child, and develop into a caring, responsible and successful adult. You will be supplying her with what she needs to face life in the adult world as an independent being, freeing her from the burden of the many social and communication stumbling blocks that might have been put in her way.

ADAPT THE COURSE TO SUIT YOUR PARTICULAR CHILD

Each parent relates differently to the different personality of his or her child. And each child in a family has a different predisposition, despite being brought up by the same parents. (One may be naturally confident while another may be naturally shy and awkward. A family tragedy or your environment may affect each in different ways – one may survive it relatively unscathed while another may not.) You will need to adapt the course to suit your particular child with her particular needs at her particular age. Your culture and religion, your social environment, your or your child's disability (and a multitude of other factors) may also play a large part in adapting the ideas to your own specific needs.

Ideally, you should read the book right through before you start the course with your child. And, should your partner be available and willing, he or she should also read the book so that you can first discuss the ideas introduced and work through any areas of conflict. This will help you both support your child through the changes she needs to make. And in making those changes, you will find that you too will need to adapt to the ideas in the course: you have to practise what you preach!

Please do not take this book as a criticism of your parenting skills. I doubt the perfect parent exists and it can be comforting to your child to know that you make some mistakes: she won't be so harsh with herself when she makes mistakes. (In fact, she would learn more if you invited her to inform you of all your social mistakes – when you are in private!) If I were the perfect parent I should not have thought of writing this book, nor felt the need to.

Professional use

Throughout the course, encourage the child to discuss what she has done with her parents and ask them to read her file and discuss the issues within it. There are also occasions throughout the course where the parent has input to the sessions, or is given a particular task to perform (identified by 'Parental Pages' and 'Task: Parents…'). Working with the parent allows the ideas introduced to be used and reinforced in the home. There is also the added advantage that small behavioural adjustments in social interactions taken into the home can benefit the whole family.

THE PROFESSIONAL AND ROLE-PLAYS

Often, hugging and kissing are suggested in the role-plays – these actions are un-avoidable since this book is about social interactions and relationships. However, it is obviously inappropriate for a professional to have close physical contact with a child in his or her care. Where hugging and kissing have been mentioned, make it clear *each time* to the child that you and she will *always* hug and kiss the air in front of each other and not actually make contact.

An alternative to this is to set up the role-play with the child's parent taking your place. The advantage of this is that the parent also learns from the role-play and can repeat it at home and adapt it for each new situation that arises.

When the role-play requires an arm or shoulder to be touched, this may be done, but ask the child's permission first, before the start of the role-play. (It is appropriate to comfort a stranger in distress with a light touch on the arm or shoulder.)

INTRODUCTION TO CHAPTER 2

If you are using this book as a professional, it is vital to work with the parent on Chapter 2, because it is the parent who has the most influence on the child's self-image and on whom the child is most dependent for affection and regard. The information pages given above can be photocopied for parents so that they can build their child's self-esteem as part of everyday life.

Ideally, the parent would be present throughout the tasks in Chapter 2, as he or she has so much input. It would be much easier if parent and professional could work together with the child during this time. However, if this is not possible, it would be useful to find out the following from the parents, to enable you to carry out the given tasks:

- What are the positive and negative things they think about their child?
- What rewards do they use or think appropriate for particular positive behaviour in their child?
- What are the limits of negative behaviour they accept in their child? What things get punished and in what way?

Read through all of Chapter 2 before attempting any tasks with a child.

Chapter 2

Improving a Child's Self-Esteem

This training course starts from within the child, so that she grows outwards, while getting to know her inner self. For lasting personal development, a child needs to see things from her own perspective, with the knowledge of the world and herself that she already has. Your help will enable the child to understand herself and the world in a more complete way and gain the skills she needs to find, eventually, her own way through.

The child needs to understand who she is and what her strengths and weaknesses are so that she builds up a complete picture of herself, knowing herself intimately. Vulnerability in her self-esteem will become evident when she is carrying out the tasks, enabling you to help improve it.

Task: Who Am I?

Ask the child the following questions and write her answers in her file.

Who am I?

SUGGESTIONS

- The daughter/son of…
- An eight-year-old.
- A child who lives in the country/town.
- A child who lives with…

What do I look like?

Things I enjoy doing

SUGGESTIONS

- Swimming.
- Dancing.
- Maths.
- Playing on the computer.
- Playing with my pet.
- Playing with my friends.
- Playing with my toys.
- Listening to stories on tape.
- Going to school.
- Going out with a friend.
- Having a friend over.
- Having a friend to stay the night.
- Staying over at my friend's house.
- Going on holiday.
- Having cuddles in bed.
- Sleeping with Mummy when Daddy's away.
- Making cards for people.
- Talking to my grandparents over the 'phone.
- Going out with my parents.
- Going to the cinema/theatre.

How I would describe myself
(Actual answers from a seven-year-old child.)

POSITIVE THINGS ABOUT MYSELF	NEGATIVE THINGS ABOUT MYSELF
• Lovely.	• Shy.
• Sweet.	• A bit aggressive.
	• Scared of things (like the dark and being shouted at).

Self-Esteem

When a child feels bad about herself, for whatever reason, her behaviour is negatively affected and her self-esteem is poor. This section is concerned with improving a child's self-esteem.

A child's self-esteem is concerned with how she values herself, or her feeling of self-worth. It is to do with how she *sees herself* and how she thinks *others see her* (her parents, siblings, other relatives, friends, teachers, religious leader, etc.). She may have a poor self-esteem if she believes other people think negative things about her. The most important person in a child's life is usually her main carer: often her mother.

Task: My Self-Esteem

Ask the child what she thinks her parents think of her. If she finds this difficult, you could help her with ideas, but she must make up her own mind. You can always add things if she thinks of other descriptions later. She must later be told what her parents actually do think of her.

Alternative: Ask the child what she thinks you, instead of her parents, think of her and progress as outlined below. (However, this would be difficult if you do not know the child well.)

What I think my parents think of me
(Actual answers from a seven-year-old child.)

POSITIVE THINGS

- A good worker.
- Good at reading.
- Good at writing.

NEGATIVE THINGS

- A bit aggressive.
- A worrier.

What my parents actually think of me
(Actual answers from the seven-year-old child's parent.)

POSITIVE THINGS

- A hard worker.
- Good at reading.
- Good at writing.
- Good at drawing.
- Lovely.
- Sweet.
- Cuddly.
- Affectionate.
- Funny.
- Clever.
- Has a generous nature.
- Talented, musically.
- Lively.
- Has a good sense of humour.
- Enjoys fun things.
- Laughs a great deal.
- Loves jokes and surprises.

NEGATIVE THINGS

- A bit aggressive.
- A worrier.
- Lazy when effort is needed.
- Rude (as in ill mannered).

Above, there are four negative comments about the child and 17 positive comments. Point out the imbalance to the child (try to make it a positive imbalance) so that the overall picture of herself is positive. (Note whether she has more negative than positive ways to describe herself, as in the above example. Then point out all the extra positive things she really has about her, to shift the balance of image from a negative to a positive one.)

Mention that you are going to use the negative points later, to work on ('Task: Parents: Tackling Your Child's Negative Behaviour').

How does having all these good things thought about you make you feel?

What do your friends like about you?

SUGGESTIONS

- I make them laugh.
- I join in with their games.
- I'm not mean to them.

Things I can do

SUGGESTIONS

- Play the piano.
- Skip.
- Tie shoelaces.
- Ride a bike.
- Skateboard.
- Swim.
- Handstands and cartwheels.
- Read and write.

- Play nicely with younger children.
- Sing.
- Make friends.
- Help someone when they are in trouble.
- Speak another language.
- Use a computer.
- Sew.
- Paint and draw.
- Bake a cake.
- Make cards.
- Play football.
- Play pool or snooker.
- Catch a ball.
- Remember people's 'phone numbers.
- Remember people's names.
- Share my things.
- Share my sweets.
- Understand the dangers around me.
- Laugh at some of my mistakes.
- Be prepared to try again, if I need to.

Did you realise you had so many talents?
No. (If she replies 'Yes', say that's good – she knows her own worth.)

How do you feel about yourself now?
Happy. (We hope!)

When you're pleased with yourself, what do you do?

SUGGESTIONS

- I hug myself.
- I jump up and down.
- I scream.
- I laugh.

And how do you feel?

SUGGESTIONS

- I feel happy.
- I feel proud.
- I feel good about myself.

Task: Rewards

Discuss appropriate rewards with the child so that she feels that she has some control over her life and some input as to what happens to her when she has done something praiseworthy. What rewards has she already been given? What rewards would she like?

Examples of rewards

- Extra time on the computer.
- Tea in front of the television.
- Extra pocket money.
- Staying up late.
- Playing a game with my parents.
- Getting a present.

- Having a friend to tea or to stay the night.
- Going swimming or bowling with a friend.
- Going to the cinema.
- Having a meal or snack out.
- Having a kiss and cuddle.
- Being read to.
- A visit to the library.

Now ask her to put the rewards in order, with her best reward last so that there is a gradual scale of *increasing* reward as you work down the list.

My order of rewards

SUGGESTIONS

1. Having a kiss and cuddle.
2. Staying up late.
3. Being read to.
4. Extra time on the computer.
5. Tea in front of the television.
6. Playing a game with my parents.
7. A visit to the library.
8. Extra pocket money.
9. Getting a present.
10. Having a meal or snack out.
11. Having a friend to tea or to stay the night.
12. Going to the cinema.
13. Going swimming or bowling with a friend.

✓

Parental Pages on Rewards and Behaviour

Photocopiable for professional use within the institution that bought the book, to use to help parents reduce their child's negative behaviour.

Note for parents on rewards

Having a tiered system of rewards allows you to give a reward in line with what your child has achieved, and one with which she agrees. However, it is important that the rewards she chooses are possible and that you are prepared to give them. If for some reason a chosen reward is not going to be used, you need to explain why not to your child and an alternative should be discussed.

If there is a regular need for reward for one particular skill or behaviour your child is trying to improve upon, have predetermined rewards for each level of achievement. For example, each time your child moves onto a new level at school, she could be rewarded, which would help her want to succeed again and have another positive experience. (Or she might have learnt to say polite things to people without having to be prompted.) Perhaps your child could choose an inexpensive gift or a book, either from a shop or a library, so that she can enjoy it with you. Or do something with her as a treat.

Be careful that, when you reward your child, you always remember to give her praise and hugs and kisses. It is extremely important to a child to have parental approval and simply presenting her with a present without mentioning what it's for or how proud you are of her does not have the same value as a gift presented with emotional warmth. The present or treat is intended to reinforce the good things you say about her, not to replace them.

An alternative approach to rewards is, instead of giving gifts, making a wall chart on which to monitor your child's progress with stars. You could have a tiered level of rewards using coloured stars for the first level, silver stars for the second and gold stars for the third and best. The chart method is particularly useful when there is an ongoing problem or weakness. For example, if your child usually forgets to greet people (saying 'Hello', 'Goodbye' and 'Thank you for having me'), she could earn a star each time she remembers.

Task: Parents: Positive Behaviour

This task is for parents to do with the help of the professional.

If a child regularly gets praised for the good things she does, she will blossom and thrive, secure in the knowledge that she is loved and valued and is pleasing to her parents. Positive behaviour should always be rewarded in some way, however small.

Discuss with your child what behaviour is positive and what she'd like you to say when she exhibits positive behaviour. Below are some ideas. If she finds it hard to think up situations herself, use these. You may also use the example responses given, but discuss them first. Your child may think of a more suitable response.

Examples of positive behaviour and appropriate responses

1. Child's behaviour: I didn't throw a wobbly when I didn't get my own way.

    Adult response: I'm proud of you for not throwing a tantrum.

2. Child's behaviour: I explained in a calm way why I didn't agree with you about something.

    Adult response: Your sensible approach made me listen.

3. Child's behaviour: I understand that we can't do what you promised, because of things (circumstances) that are out of your control.

    Adult response: I'm so glad you understand. How about doing…instead?

4. Child's behaviour: I was patient with a younger child who didn't know how to behave towards me.

    Adult response: I'm proud of you for putting up with a younger child who's been pestering you.

5. Child's behaviour: I told you about someone's bullying behaviour towards me.

   Adult response: Thank you for telling me. I'm glad you can protect yourself in this way. Now I'll let Mrs X know so that this person is stopped from doing it to you again and, we hope, to others too. No one has a right to bully you.

6. Child's behaviour: I am polite when Grandma visits me, remembering to kiss her and say, 'Thank you.'

   Adult response: It makes me proud when I see how polite you are to others.

7. Child's behaviour: I didn't fuss when you pulled the splinter out of my hand.

   Adult response: I'm glad you kept still so that I could get the splinter out whole – you were very brave.

8. Child's behaviour: I reminded you that the time of your favourite programme had been changed.

   Adult response: Thank you for thinking about me and letting me know. I would have been disappointed to have missed Eastenders.

9. Child's behaviour: I understood not to say something so that you weren't embarrassed.

   Adult response: It was very clever of you to realise not to say anything. Thank you.

10. Child's behaviour: I didn't laugh when Grandpa spilt food down himself.

    Adult response: I'm proud of you for not laughing at Grandpa and for understanding that some old people make a mess when they eat and drink.

Try to avoid using the terms good and bad behaviour because your child may think that these words also apply to her – she is good when she has done something positive but bad when she has done something negative. A child is neither good nor bad through her behaviour. She is always the same, her behaviour does not affect this.

When your child does wrong, it is her behaviour that must be addressed, not her personally. For example, if she drops something and it breaks, don't say 'You're clumsy' but 'That was clumsy of you.' It is important to remember this so that situations don't become hostile and spiral out of control.

Examples of addressing the behaviour, not the person

You idiot!	*Why did you do that?*
You plonker!	*That was a silly thing to do.*
You're useless.	*You need more practice.*
I hate you!	*I hate it when you do that.*
You're a disappointment.	*I'm disappointed that you did that.*
You're shameful.	*I didn't expect that of you.*
You liar!	*I don't like it when you lie.*

NOTE

Only *negative* comments aimed at someone personally damage her self-esteem. Your child will not feel hurt or offended if you say to her 'You're brilliant!' when she's just got her BAGA 6 gymnastics award. You don't have to worry about getting your wording right here. It's better than saying, 'You're very good at gymnastics.' Praise can, and should, be lavish when it is deserved.

Try not to compare your child with other children and think that her achievements are not worth much because all her friends can do the same and more. How your child manages to improve herself must be praised, regardless of how she does compared to her peers.

Task: Parents: Dealing with Negative Behaviour

This task is for parents to do with the help of the professional. (Once the limits of behaviour in each category have been decided upon, discuss them with the child.)

In addition to ensuring that negative comments are directed at your child's behaviour rather than herself, there needs to be a clear idea of the limits for unacceptable behaviour. Is your child aware of these limits? If she isn't, she does not have a secure framework within which to live and may often be confused about why some behaviour reaps drastic disciplinary measures while other behaviour does not.

Write a list of the limits of unacceptable behaviour in your child's file, using the categories given below. The given suggestions are to help you with ideas. Once you have decided on the limits, openly discuss them with your child. (Your list can always be amended later, by adding or removing an entry or changing an entry from one category to another.)

Totally unacceptable behaviour

This should always be pointed out to your child as close to the event as possible and should *always* result in some form of punishment or denial of something.

- Being rude to people outside the family.
- Showing your parents up, for example, by throwing a huge wobbly in public.
- Deliberately misbehaving when you know your parents are powerless to correct you in the situation they are in.
- Damaging something valuable through an action you'd been previously warned about.
- Answering your parents back.
- Being very rude to your parents.

General negative behaviour

This is *always* brought to your child's attention but might not always be punished. She might be told how disappointed you are in her and that it must not happen again. She might be warned about what would happen if she repeats the offence.

- Not co-operating with your parents when they, or you, have guests, and taking advantage of your parents' wish of not wanting to make a scene.

- Refusing to do something you're asked.

- Forgetting to thank someone for having you or for being given a present.

- Humming a tune while your parents are trying to talk to you.

- Being caught out in a biggish lie; for example, saying you'd done your homework when you hadn't. (You may feel this is more serious and want to put it in the category above.)

Undesired behaviour

This is the least important negative behaviour and it may not always be brought to your child's attention. (Mentioning every mistake to a child lowers her self-esteem. Here, you can judge whether she will be receptive to criticism, depending on what's gone on before.)

- Doing something you've been asked to do with bad grace.

- Telling a small lie (for example, saying that you've washed your hands for tea when it's obvious you haven't).

- Complaining about doing your homework.

- Refusing to tidy your room.

- Being silly.

- Playing music too loud.

- Saying 'In a minute' when your parents have said 'Now'.
- Saying, 'Why?' whenever you are asked to do something.

Children can never be perfect and you sometimes need to let things go or your child will be constantly criticised. If your child's behaviour is predominantly in the first category, concentrate on improving this before addressing lesser problems. Too high expectations of behaviour can damage her self-esteem and she may lose all desire even to try to improve her behaviour, seeing it as an impossible task.

What aspects of your child's behaviour are most troubling? Work on a reward system with your child's agreement to try to overcome this difficulty before passing on to the next, using the ideas above.

Task: Parents: Tackling Your Child's Negative Behaviour

This task is for parents to do with the help of the professional.

You can help improve your child's self-esteem by addressing her negative qualities. You can help her reduce the number of occasions negative behaviour occurs, and the degree of her negative behaviour, by suggesting alternative behaviour. This will reduce the number of times she (and you) feels bad, improving her self-esteem.

Look back to the child's negative behaviour comments (at the beginning of Chapter 2) and write a main heading for each in her file. The examples given were: A worrier; Lazy when effort is needed; Rude (as in ill mannered); and Aggressive. Bullying has also been added to the list as it is a very common negative behaviour problem.

Under each heading, think up techniques for you to use to help your child overcome the following problem areas. Then discuss them with her and ask her to remind you about the ways in which you can help when necessary. Some suggestions follow.

A worrier

- Try to encourage your child without pushing her.
- Support her.
- Listen to her fears.
- If you can give practical help, do. (For example, by telling her teacher if she is being bullied; by arranging for a friend to go with her to a party rather than arriving on her own; by helping her with her homework or with revising for a test.)
- Discuss her fears with people who could help her, with her permission if possible. This may be her teacher or her friends.
- Be gentle but firm when there are things she has to do. (For example, worries about attending school.)
- Get professional help if you feel the problem is beyond you and it is interfering with your child's life. (For example, school phobia or Obsessive Compulsive Disorder.)
- Ask your friends for advice – they may have gone through the same thing.
- Allow her to do things in her own time (within reason). Ensure that time is available for this. (Get up earlier if necessary.) Reward her if there is time to spare by allowing her to do something she likes before she leaves, or before the expected event occurs, such as watching television.
- Ensure your child is never late for school, an outing, or an appointment, as this will make her worry. If her home life

is well organised and under control, she will feel more secure, knowing she can rely on you, trusting you to make things all right.

- If things don't go according to plan, don't show panic or worry yourself, as this will unnerve her. Be calm and talk through any problems that arise and explain how you are going to make things right.

Lazy when effort is needed

- Explain to your child that there are some things she must do and may as well accept that they are a part of life, either in school or at home. They are non-negotiable.

- Be understanding. ('I know you find this hard but...')

- Ease her burden by helping. Could you do it together or explain how she could make it easier for herself?

- Split up big tasks into smaller goals. For example, instead of demanding she tidies an extremely messy room that minute say, 'Tidy your floor now and then we'll have lunch. After lunch you can tidy your bed and surfaces and then you can watch...')

- Offer rewards for completing tasks within the limits you've set.

- Give rewards for larger tasks. For example, if she manages to make her handwriting neater.

- Reward all achievements in some way to make her proud of herself and encourage her to want more rewards and approval.

- Let her see you verbally reward other people when they have done something noteworthy but don't ever compare her to any other person. Never say, 'Well, Jason's already done it so I don't see why you can't.' This will make her want to rebel and she will feel bad about herself. Positive approaches give positive behaviour.

- If you must compare, compare her with herself six months or a year ago. For example, you could say, 'Your writing used to be much neater than this. I expect it to get better, not worse.'

Rude (as in ill mannered)

- Explain that being rude does not make life easy for her – she gets punished and you get angry.

- Point out how proud you are of her when she's polite.

- Warn her that people may not like her as much if she is rude to them.

- Help her to find alternatives to her rudeness. For example, instead of lashing out by saying 'I hate you' she could say, 'That's not fair because…' This would get her a better result and spare her, and your, feelings.

- Tell her she can't expect you to co-operate with her if she is rude to you. Ask her how she would feel if you were rude to her. Would she want to do something for you under that circumstance?

- Tell her what sort of things you'd like her to say and when. For example, 'Please may I leave the table?' when she's finished her meal.

- Remind her of your expectations before certain situations. For example, before she goes to someone's house, remind her that you expect her to thank the person for having her and to remember to be polite at the table.

- If you know she is going to be bored in a certain situation, think of things to divert her attention. Could she take a jigsaw, comic or book to read with her? Or some drawing things? Or could you make a private arrangement to sweeten the pill of having to visit, for example, an elderly relative, such as buying her an ice cream on the way home?

- Explain that, as well as saying the right words, she has to look right too: it's no good saying 'Hello' to someone without giving a smile of welcome.

Aggressive (See also Chapter 10, 'Anger')

- In what ways is she aggressive? (Stroppy? Sticking her tongue out? Calling people rude names? Shouting? Answering back? Hitting, biting or pinching?)

- How does she feel when she is aggressive? Is this how she likes to feel?

- What effect does she think it has on others? (How do they feel about themselves and her? How do they behave towards her?)

- Discuss what happens to her when she is aggressive. (Does she get what she wants? Is she punished? Was it worth while in any way?)

- What could she do instead? (Count to ten? Leave the room to cool off and return when she can calmly discuss the matter with you? Ask herself if her behaviour is reasonable – whether she'd like it if you treated her in this way.)

- Ask her to try to limit her aggressive behaviour to situations that warrant it – for example, if she's been promised a treat that is later denied because of changing circumstances, it would be understandable for her to be really upset. Perhaps she needs understanding rather than punishment at this time. ('I know you're disappointed and I'm sorry that you are upset, but there's nothing we can do about it. We had no way of knowing that…')

- Explain that she can stand up for herself without being aggressive. For example, she could say 'I don't agree with you because…' and you'd be more likely to listen and might be persuaded to change your mind if she's pointed out something you hadn't thought of. Or it might be that your child didn't thoroughly understand the situation, so talking it through helps her accept it, realising it is out of your hands.

Bullying

- Find out why your child bullies.
- How does she think the bullied people feel?
- How does she feel? Is that a good way to feel?
- Is she proud of her behaviour?
- Check that your child isn't being bullied or over-pressured at home or that something negative isn't going on, such as suffering some form of abuse. ('Has something happened to upset you?')
- How could she make things better with those she's bullied?
- Is there any way you could help change her behaviour by changing yours? (Are you too strict with her? Do you bully her? Are you violent towards her? Does she feel frustrated and resentful about something you've done?)
- Help her to make amends. Take her to the bullied person's home, if possible, and persuade her to apologise.

It is important for parents not to reward negative behaviour. For example, if your child throws a wobbly because she was told 'No', you must not give in. Otherwise, your child will see it as a worthwhile ploy to manipulate you and she will make it even harder for you to refuse next time. Eventually, she will not take what you say seriously. This will leave you feeling bad and your child with the wrong ideas about acceptable behaviour.

Children also need a good role model. If you throw a wobbly, it will be difficult to persuade your child that her behaviour is unacceptable.

Task: How to Avoid Big Trouble

Discuss with the child occasions when she's got into *big* trouble. Write them down in her file and discuss and record the consequences using the headings given below. (An example situation has been given.)

The importance of this exercise is for the child to understand the consequences of negative behaviour, the reasons for punishment and how people feel when such things happen.

What happened?

I played catch with a vase and dropped it. It broke. I'd been told before not to play with it but I didn't take any notice.

What sort of trouble was I in?

I got sent to bed early and was not allowed a tape to listen to. And I lost my pocket money.

Why were my parents so angry?

- Because I'd been told not to touch their things before and I knew it wasn't a toy.
- Because they gave me warnings and I didn't listen.
- Because it was worth a lot.
- Because they were tired and it was the last straw. I'd done other silly things that day.

When a child gets into trouble, check that she understands why. If she doesn't, she does not learn from the experience and will be hurt and confused, finding it harder to take responsibility for what she's done. (Ask the child's parents to check her understanding of the situation.)

What sort of punishments do I get?

- I lose my pocket money.
- I can't watch television.
- I'm told to leave the room.
- A trip out is cancelled.
- I get sent to bed early.
- I'm not allowed on the computer.
- I get shouted at.
- I can't go out to play with my friends.

Smacking as a punishment has been omitted as many parents are opposed to it and it is only acceptable in other quarters if the force is controlled and the child is not damaged by it. Whenever possible, a punishment that deprives the child of some looked-for pleasure is preferable, since it does not physically harm the child.

Put the punishments in order, with the biggest last

SUGGESTIONS

1. I get shouted at.
2. I'm told to leave the room.
3. I'm not allowed on the computer.
4. I can't watch television.
5. I get sent to bed early.
6. I lose my pocket money.
7. I can't go out to play with my friends.
8. A trip out is cancelled.

How to observe warnings

Can the child remember times when she knew she would be in big trouble before she'd actually done the thing?

SUGGESTIONS

- When I was warned just beforehand.
- When I was asked to stop but carried on.
- When I remembered I'd been told off about it before.
- When my dad was tired and he told me he was.
- When I'd been warned that time was short and I'd need to hurry.
- When I'd been told to pay attention because my dad had got something important to explain to me.
- When my dad's face and voice looked and sounded very angry.

Children should be given warning of an impending punishment or admonishment. For example, a child should be told that if she repeats the offence one more time such and such will happen.

Ask the child to try to remember the absolute no-nos of behaviour so that her parents don't have to get so angry with her and she doesn't have to feel so bad about it afterwards. With her parents reminding her of what is expected of her, and her listening and seeing the warning signs, great improvements in behaviour should ensue.

Conclusion

Parents can work with a child to improve her self-esteem in a variety of ways. This does not mean that they fail to discipline her when necessary, but it does mean that the discipline they mete out should be commensurate with the wrong-doing.

Parents should praise their child whenever they can, show her as much love and affection as they can and spend time with her. They should show understanding of her faults, accept they themselves have faults too, and should work together with their child to overcome them. They should not have too high expectations. None of us is perfect.

Boosting a child's self-esteem should be ongoing. She needs love and support throughout her life and there is no one better equipped to give this than her parent.

Chapter 3

Friends

It is important for everyone to have friends. Children's friends are people from outside the home whom a child does things with – plays with, goes out with, talks to and shares problems with. A child can be helped to make friends using the social skills developed from this course and by parents providing the opportunities for her to mix outside her school and home environment. (For example, if all the children she sits with in school socialise with one another outside school, and she doesn't, they are more likely to have strong bonds among themselves but not with her.)

Should the child not attend school, for whatever reason, it is even more important for her to be provided with social opportunities so that she gains support from friendships and increases her self-esteem, knowing others value her. She can also practise what she learns from this course, to improve her social skills and increase her confidence in dealing with others.

Other relationships are dealt with later in the book.

Task: All about Friends

Add these questions and the child's answers to the child's file. Suggestions have been given where appropriate.

What are friends?

- Other children I like and enjoy being with.
- Other children I care about.

- Other children about the same age as me. (Adult friendships tend to be more diverse and can accommodate vast age differences.)
- Children I have things in common with (we go to the same school, live near each other, go to the same clubs).
- Children I do things with: those I play with, go to clubs with, watch television with and go out with.
- Children who listen to what I have to say.
- Children I share my good news with and who listen when I'm sad.
- Children I share my things with.

Why are friends important?

- I would be lonely without them.
- We need to help one another.
- They are people I can relax with, without them telling me off. They don't mind about things like adults.
- I can be silly with them.
- I can play with them for ages without them getting bored, like my parents might.
- They are about the same age as me, are interested in similar things and we have fun together.
- They can help me when I'm sad or scared.
- We can play interesting games when there are lots of us.
- I can sometimes tell them things I wouldn't tell my own parents.
- They help look after me.
- I can learn from them and they from me.

Who are my friends?

What do I like about them?
- They are good fun.
- They are funny and make me laugh.
- They are lively and exciting to be with.
- We share things.
- They are nice to me.
- I enjoy being with them.
- They comfort me when I'm sad.
- They look after me when I hurt myself or feel ill.

How do your friends behave towards you?
- They look pleased to see me.
- They seek me out.
- They hug me.
- They tell me if I'm doing something wrong.
- Sometimes they shut me out.
- They let me borrow things.
- They explain things when I don't understand.
- They laugh at me when I do something silly.
- They tell me jokes.
- They make me 'Get Well' cards when I'm very ill.
- They help me celebrate my birthday.
- They send me postcards when they're on holiday.

How do you behave towards them?
- I look pleased to see them.
- I seek them out.

- I lend them things.
- I smile when I see them. I sometimes hug them.
- I remind them about things they need to know or do.
- I warn them when they are doing something wrong or dangerous.
- I explain things to them when they don't understand.
- I show them my new toys and let them play with them.
- I share my sweets and crisps with them.
- I make them cards for birthdays and getting well.
- I send them postcards when I'm on holiday.
- I help them when they are in trouble.
- I get help for them when they've hurt themselves or don't feel well.

Task: Keeping Friends

This section consists of example situations where friendship is put at risk. Discuss with the child what she would do in each case, giving reasons. (She needs to understand the possible consequences of certain actions.)

Example 1

You see your friend still talking when your teacher has asked you all to be quiet and listen. What do you do?

(a) Nothing.

(b) Tell your friend to stop talking.

(c) Try to catch your friend's eye and put your finger to your lips.

Option (a) is something an uncaring friend would do: nothing – and let the person get into trouble. Option (b) might get you into trouble for talking yourself. The teacher might, at that moment, glance up and catch you. Option (c) is the best choice since no verbal interaction takes place. If you sit next to your friend, you could nudge her to catch her attention and then put your finger to your lips. Or you could gently kick her under the table. If she's too far away, you could try to get her attention by waving your hand at her. Then you could put your finger to your lips or make a head movement in the direction of your teacher.

Example 2

Your friend has a phobia (a terrible fear) of spiders. She sees one by her desk and shows it to you. What do you do?

(a) Laugh.

(b) Pick it up and put it in her bag.

(c) Comfort and reassure her.

Option (a) is unkind. A caring friend would never laugh at her or make fun of her fear, even if she could not understand it herself. Option (b) is also unkind. A caring friend would not pick it up and put it on her or in her bag. Option (c) is the friendliest. Comfort her and reassure her. Then remove the spider yourself or get someone else to do it.

Example 3

You have been invited to Pete's house for tea. But then Shaun invites you to something better. What do you do?

(a) Ask Pete about it and ask if he minds if you go round to his house another time.

(b) Tell Pete that you no longer want to go to his house – you're going out with Shaun.

(c) Refuse Shaun's offer and explain that you've already agreed to go to Pete's house.

Option (a) might offend Pete, but not as much as option (b) would. Option (b) gives a clear message that you much prefer Shaun to Pete. This would hurt Pete's feelings and make him feel angry and resentful towards you and Shaun. Option (c) is the best to go for if you want to be sure of staying friends with Pete.

Task: Friendship Groups

Discuss the child's friendship group with her. Write the questions and the child's answers in the child's file.

Do you have a best friend?

If you do, what's special about her?

Who are your other friends?

Are there any friends you play with occasionally, outside this group?

Write the following questions and the child's own answers in the child's file.

It is important to have many friends. Why do you think that is?

- If you fall out with your best friend, you'll still have others to play with.
- If your best friend is away from school for a long time, you'll have other children to play with and do things with.
- If you only have one friend and she's away or leaves the school, there'll be no one special and you might feel unhappy about going to school and you might not enjoy it so much.
- Different friends may enjoy doing different things. If you have many friends, you might choose to play football with one, play on the computer with another, draw and colour with a third and play made-up games with a fourth. That way, every part of you can be satisfied.
- Different friends have a variety of different strengths. One may be good at listening to your problems; another may be good at

getting you to exercise; another to get you to laugh. This helps to keep you and your interests balanced.

- With many friends, you come across many more difficult situations and you learn far more about human nature. This helps make you a more skilled friend yourself.

- Having many friends adds to your feeling of security and boosts your self-esteem.

- It's more fun to have many friends. And, if you are all friends together, you can play more interesting and involved games.

What things break up a friendship?

- Telling your friend's secret.
- Telling lies about your friend.
- Deliberately trying to get your friend into trouble.
- Being rude and horrible to your friend and not apologising and explaining after.
- Hurting your friend – physically or emotionally (hurting her feelings).
- If your friend does all the hard work – if she always calls you or invites you round – it looks as though you don't care as much about her as she cares about you. The friendship needs to be balanced, with each of you sharing the running.
- Being the one who always tags along, needing support and never being able to give support yourself. This makes the relationship unbalanced and unrewarding to your friend.
- Being jealous of the time your friend spends with others. She does not belong to you and you must allow her the freedom to mix with other people as she must allow you the same freedom.

Task: Making New Friends

When a child first meets someone, it may be hard to get the relationship going. She or the other person might be too shy to make it progress or even get started. Typical situations where a child has the opportunity to make friends are when:

- she goes to a new school
- someone new starts at her school
- she joins a new club (swimming, gymnastics, football, karate)
- she goes on holiday and there's a children's club to join
- she goes to special religious classes or events
- she joins a youth club.

Write the following questions and the child's answers in the child's file.

What can you do to make friends with someone?

- Go up and say 'Hello'.
- Ask the person's name.
- Tell her your name.
- Ask her something to do with the place you're in such as: 'Is this your first time at the club?' 'Have you been camping before?' 'Where was your old school?' 'Why did you change school?'
- Give information at the same level about yourself. For example, if she tells you how old she is, tell her your age.
- Offer to do something for the person. For example, you could offer to show her round the school, sit by her at lunch, share a toy or invite her to join in your game.
- Ask her to help you in some way. ('Can you help me do…?') Then you can start chatting – about what you need help with, and later other things too.

What things might stop the friendship from going further?

- If you treat her badly or behave inappropriately towards her.
- If she makes fun of you.
- If you find out she's done something dreadful and you strongly disapprove.
- Your parents might not like something about her and stop you from seeing her outside school.
- Her parents might not like something about you and stop her from seeing you outside school.
- Your teacher might think she's a bad influence on you and tell your parents about it. They might try to stop the friendship.
- She might use you – be friends with you when it suits her, but dropping you as soon as someone else comes along.
- She might hurt you in some way.
- You are too embarrassed for her to see your home so never invite her round.
- You might be embarrassed about one or both of your parents because of the problems they have or how they live their life, and you don't want her to find out so never invite her home.
- You might not be allowed out with your friends without an adult from your own culture to chaperone you.
- You might not be allowed to go to discos or parties and so you are left out from a large chunk of what your friends talk about.

Task: Honesty in Friendships

Deeper friendships result if a child can be honest with her friends. This means sometimes admitting she has a problem or a weakness, and entrusting her friend with this valuable piece of information. This encourages her friend to match this honesty so that the two of them get to know one another better, strengthening their friendship.

How honest would the child be in the following exercises? Discuss the situations and the pros and cons of each option.

Exercise 1

You and your friend both entered the school poetry competition. Your friend won first prize. Your entry didn't get placed (it wasn't second or third). What do you say to your friend when you find out?

(a) 'I'm so pleased for you, well done. My entry didn't get placed.'

(b) 'They couldn't have read my poem properly.'

(c) 'Well done. I wish I'd won something too.'

Option (c) will make the other person feel uncomfortable about winning, although it is honest. Option (b) shows pure jealousy and is the worst of the lot. Option (a) is the most socially skilful as you congratulate your friend and then simply state what happened about your poem without making your friend feel bad about winning.

Exercise 2

Your friend admits to feeling scared about going away with the Scouts for the first time. This will be your first time away and you feel nervous too. What do you say to him?

(a) You laugh and say, 'Don't be such a baby!'

(b) You are scornful and say, 'Haven't you been away before?'

(c) You say, 'Me too. But we'll be together.'

Options (a) and (b) are both aggressive answers as they make the friend feel bad about himself. Option (b) is also downright dishonest as it implies that you are used to going away and that you aren't nervous. Option (c) is honest and reassuring.

Exercise 3

A group of you are out in town together. Some of them find out that your friend, who is also present, is not allowed to parties where the parents aren't at home and laugh at her. Your parents have the same rule. Do you admit to it and risk being laughed at?

(a) You join in with the laughter.

(b) You admit to your parents having the same rules and invite them to laugh at you too.

(c) You tell them there's nothing wrong with parents having rules about parties – it's a sensible idea.

Option (a) is dishonest and you probably won't be proud of your behaviour afterwards, nor will your friend be too chuffed with you. Option (c) is better but cowardly. The others will probably guess that your parents have the same rule and, even if not, if your friend knows or finds out she won't be too pleased with you. Option (b) is the hardest to say but will win you respect. You can't help your parents' rules and therefore should not be judged on them by your friends.

Task: Being Tactful

There are times when a child should *not* be completely honest. This is when her honesty would unnecessarily hurt her friend. If skirting around the truth a little would do no lasting harm, the extra trouble a child takes will show sensitivity towards another and will smooth over the difficult area.

The following exercises are on tact. Discuss the situations with the child and the pros and cons of each option. (Tact is looked at again in Chapter 11.)

Exercise 1

Someone who joins your class has a large red birthmark on her face. What do you do when you meet her?

(a) Stare fixedly at the mark.

(b) Say, 'What happened to your face?'

(c) Do your best to ignore it and concentrate on the conversation.

Options (a) and (b) are rude and unfeeling. This person has had to live with the mark for years and must be thoroughly fed up with everyone staring at it. Option (b) is demanding personal information from her before she may be ready to give it. Option (c) is tactful. If you get on with the person, then ask her about the mark – she may be glad to tell you once she knows you're sympathetic towards her so that she can get the inevitable questions over with.

Exercise 2

You are given a game for your birthday, but you already have it. What do you do?

(a) Thank the person very nicely.

(b) Say, 'Oh. Thanks.'

(c) Say, 'Oh, I've already got it!'

Option (c) is completely tactless. You are throwing the person's present back into his face, telling him it's no good for you and that you don't want it. This is a harsh way to treat someone when he is doing you a favour and can't be expected to know he didn't guess right about the present. Option (b) is a bit flat. The giver will feel hurt and think you don't appreciate him or the effort he's gone to. Option (a) is the kindest. (You can sort out what to do about the present later, with your parents.)

Exercise 3

Your friend has just had his eyebrow pierced and you think it's gross. What do you say when you first see it?

(a) 'That's great!'

Child: You are secretly pleased as you cannot stand the girl and she has often tried to bully you. But you must hide your pleasure at hearing what has happened to the girl, or her mother will be offended and angry. You must show concern.

Secretly scared

Adult: You have been bullying a child and come across the child in the park on her way home. You decide to block her path.

Child: You are scared of the other child but you must not look it. Bullies like to scare people and you would be playing into his or her hands if you show what you really feel. Look the person straight in the eye.

One area that children would love to be able to fool us over is trying to hide the fact that they are lying. This has been omitted from the course as it would be teaching the child negative behaviour. Also, parents need to know what is going on in their child's life in order to understand them and help them (and know what the truth is). You could, however, point out that people often blush when they lie as this cannot be controlled through willpower. Lying is not positive social behaviour and can only be excused when it is used to keep the child safe. (This does not refer to 'white' lies that have many worthy uses – tact being one of them: see Chapter 11, 'Task: Tact').

Another favourite is pretending to be asleep. Children tend to get quite skilled at this themselves. Parents also like to pretend they are still asleep early in the morning in the hope of getting a few extra minutes in bed.

Cultural differences in social behaviour

Depending on what culture a child is from, there are different body language and social expectations. Parents should explain to their child how they expect her to behave at home and how they expect her to behave outside the home when she is mixing with other cultures.

For example, if a child is from a Latin American country, she would be much more physical with people: touching and hugging and standing very close. This would be appropriate in her home with people from the same background but not in, say, British society where people rarely touch and don't stand at all close. (This does not mean she should be encouraged to have friendships with little or no emotional warmth or physical contact.)

One is expected to look the person in the eye when talking to a Westerner, yet in the Far East, many women avoid eye contact to show humility. When greeting a good friend in the West, often hugs or kisses are expected, yet in the Far East often just words are more appropriate.

Also, in the Far East, it is often expected to refuse something offered and wait for it to be offered a second or third time before graciously accepting. In Western society, we might take someone at his or her word and not think to offer again once something was refused. In some Far Eastern cultures, modesty is valued so highly it might be inappropriate to tell someone of your achievements whereas in Western culture, people are encouraged to share good news with their friends. Compliments may also be initially rejected by Far Easterners, denying that they possess that particular asset or insisting that an achievement was just luck. In the West, such a rejection would be interpreted as being passive and exhibiting social clumsiness, since assertion and gracious acceptance of compliments are valued in the West.

A child who operates in two or more cultures needs to be more skilled at assessing what behaviour is appropriate at the time and being able to adapt her behaviour with fluidity to the current demands of the situation – no easy task! She should be reminded whenever possible of appropriate behaviour for forth-coming events so that she is prepared, increasing her social confidence and adaptability within both cultures.

Conclusion

Body language is a very complex skill to master. Often, children (and some adults) have difficulty matching what they say to the body messages they give. They should practise looking pleased when they are pleased, angry when they are angry etc., to reinforce what they say and so that they do not give conflicting spoken and body messages.

People feel uncomfortable when they deal with others who give conflicting messages because it suggests that the person is untrustworthy or unpredictable and this could hamper the development of the person's relationships. Properly tuned body language, on the other hand, can augment relationships and make them more meaningful and genuine to the other person.

Chapter 8

Assertiveness

There are generally three types of behaviour: aggressive, passive and assertive. Aggressive behaviour is to do with hurting people, making them feel bad about themselves, shouting and being angry. It is not respecting other people's rights and thinking one is better or more important than someone else. It is about being inconsiderate and always putting oneself first. It is being impatient and expecting unreasonable things.

Passive behaviour is about accepting everything and not trying to stand up for oneself or one's friends. Passive people don't try to change the way things are, they go for an easy way out and find it hard to say 'No' to something. Passive people get taken advantage of and can be easily bullied or intimidated.

Assertive behaviour is about sticking up for oneself in a way that does not hurt others, knowing when to say 'No' and telling other people when their behaviour is unreasonable. It is understanding that other people have rights too and respecting their feelings and wishes. Assertiveness is hard to achieve but consists of positive behaviour that others cannot criticise for unfairness or unreasonableness and is honest, true behaviour that does not manipulate others or put them down (such as when being sarcastic).

Task: Aggressiveness, Passivity and Assertiveness

Explain the meaning of aggressive, passive and assertive behaviour to the child. Then discuss the following:

Why might some people be aggressive?

- They are naturally aggressive.
- They have learnt to behave aggressively because their parents are aggressive.
- They are treated harshly at home, with little understanding or patience.
- They feel bad about themselves (have a low self-esteem).
- They are jealous of other people.
- They are not doing well at school and this upsets them.
- They are unhappy with how they look.
- They are unhappy with how others have treated them.
- They are spoilt and always get their own way or throw a wobbly until they do.

Why might some people be passive?

- They are naturally shy and quiet.
- They have learnt to be shy and quiet because their parents are passive.
- They do not know how to stand up for themselves.
- They have very strict parents and are mostly afraid of doing something wrong.
- They might have tried to make their viewpoint heard but since no one listened they gave up.
- They might be lazy and can't be bothered to make the effort to be better understood.

Why might some people be assertive?

- They are naturally confident and assertive (although assertive skills usually need to be learnt).

- They have seen how their parents behave, have learnt how to make their meaning clear, how to explain any misunderstandings and how to point out any unfairness.
- They are not scared to stand up for themselves.
- They have parents who listen to what they say and take them seriously.

Which group do you fall into? Why do you think this is?

It may be that you fall into more than one group. You might be aggressive with a younger sibling, passive with your best friend at school and assertive with someone else. Often your behaviour changes depending on with whom you are interacting and where. For example, you might feel more confident at a party in your own home than in a posh restaurant with a friend or in your head-teacher's office.

Assertiveness is about standing up for your rights and not letting other people take advantage of you. You need to be able to say 'No' to some people some times. (This does not mean you should repeatedly refuse reasonable requests from your parents. You need to develop the skill to decide when to give in and when to stand your ground.)

Task: Saying 'No'

There are times when a child must say 'No' to protect herself and to not let others take advantage of her. Read the following example to the child and then discuss the situation.

Example

Your friend is in trouble for writing a note in class. The teacher confiscates it and you all know he will show it to your friend's mother. He puts the note up high on a shelf. At break-time, you and your friend are left alone in the class. You are taller than your friend and she asks you to reach up and get the note for her.

You must say 'No' for the following reasons:

- If you were to get the note, your teacher will find out it's missing and if he knew you'd taken it, you'd get into trouble and he might think badly of you.

- If your teacher were to return to the room as you were reaching up for the note, you'd be in trouble too.

- The teacher has seen and read the note, so your friend cannot get out of her trouble. It would not help her even if you did take the note. It might well make things worse for her.

- Your friend must take responsibility for what she has done.

- She has no right to involve you in this.

How to behave when saying 'No'

Tell the child to use confident body language when she is saying 'No', as she has to look as though she means it. This includes:

- standing, or sitting, up straight
- facing the person squarely
- looking the person straight in the eye
- looking as though you expect your answer to be accepted
- making your voice sound firm and strong (but not loud)
- pronouncing 'No' clearly with no mumbling.

How do I say 'No'?

Discuss with the child what she should say in the following situations. The child should say 'No' and explain why to reinforce the message.

1. A friend asks to copy your homework from you. He regularly asks to do this and never wants you to help him – he just can't be bothered to do the work himself.

   Response: 'No. You've copied my work loads of times and got credit for what you didn't do. I'm not going to have you take advantage of me any more.'

2. Many of your friends have started smoking. You don't want to smoke as you know it's bad for you. One of them offers you a cigarette.

   Response: 'No thanks. I don't want to.'

   When you refuse they call you chicken.

   Response: 'It's not chicken to make my own mind up about things.'

   If they push you further, you could give a slightly aggressive response:

   Response: 'I'm not a sheep either. I don't blindly follow everyone else.'

   Or, if you wish to stay wholly assertive, keep repeating the first line 'No thanks. I don't want to' until the person gets the message.

3. A friend keeps borrowing money off you to buy sweets, but she never pays you back. She's just asked you again.

   Response: 'No, not any more. You haven't paid me back what you already owe me.'

4. A group of children from your school is standing outside the sweet shop. As you're about to go in, one of them dares you to get what you want without paying for it.

   Response: 'No. I don't think that's brave – it's stupid.'

   (Note that the child is not calling the other child stupid, but the idea of shoplifting.)

5. You walk home with a friend from school. He suggests that you take a short cut through some wasteland. Your parents have forbidden you to use that route. When you tell him this he says, 'Come on, they'll never know.'

   Response: 'No. It's a rule I was given to keep me safe. You go if you want to.'

The problems with saying 'No'

In theory, 'No' is easy to say. But when a child is with friends, it is hard to be different, hard to stand up to them, because she may feel stupid and cowardly. But a child's friends have no right to make her feel this way. If they really respect and value her, they would not put her on the spot. A child should only do things she wants to do and believes in. Many believe it is not 'cool' to refuse to join in – but it actually is much 'cooler' for a child to make her own decisions and be her own person.

Many children start smoking from a very young age, before they even really consider what might happen in the future. Is it 'cool', for example, for a child to be addicted to cigarettes before she is out of her teens or to be dependent on non-medicinal drugs? Is it 'cool' to steal or bully?

Anything that a child does that she does not wholeheartedly believe in lowers her self-esteem and she loses her sense of self. Other people are dictating how she should behave. A child should be the master of her own thoughts and body.

Task: Standing up for, and Protecting, Others

Throughout a child's life, she will see injustices done. A shy person may not feel able to do anything about it, but if she discusses unfair situations with you, she may be able to think up ways in which to overcome her shyness and intervene on behalf of someone less able to speak up.

Discuss with the child what she should do or say in the following situations. Practising standing up for others will give her confidence to act independently in real life.

1. A new pupil starts at your school. She dresses differently to everyone else and the other children have started to make fun of her.

    Response: 'Don't be so mean. She can't help what she's dressed in.'

    Or: 'Would you be mean to me if I were dressed like that? It wouldn't make any difference to me if you were dressed like that.'

2. You see someone being robbed in the street.

   Response: Run away and find help in a nearby shop or public area. (You should never try to stop a thief yourself as you might get hurt. This is particularly true for children.)

3. You are on a country walk with a young cousin or brother. He decides to wander off in a different direction. The adults are some way ahead of you and haven't noticed.

   Response: Don't go with him; you might both end up being lost without anyone knowing where either you or he is. If you can't persuade him to stay on the same path, shout to one of the adults immediately. It is not your responsibility to keep a younger child safe by going off without permission from, or the knowledge of, the adults caring for you.

4. You overhear an argument between children at your school. Three children have ganged up against one other, saying that he's lying. He insists that what he's said is true. You know it is too. You heard it on the radio that morning.

   Response: 'He's telling the truth. I heard it on the radio this morning. It really is true.'

5. Your friend gets a chain letter, threatening all sorts of horrible things if she doesn't send off seven more letters saying the same things to people she knows within ten days. The letter has frightened her.

   Response: 'Ignore it. Tear it up and throw it away. Words on paper can't hurt you.'

   Or: 'Give it to your parents. They'll tear it up for you. Or let me do it. Someone's just being really nasty. You can't possibly upset seven others the way this letter has upset you. It's all nonsense anyway.'

Task: Protecting Yourself

There is nothing chicken about a child protecting herself. It is actually more cowardly to go with the flow instead of making one's own decisions and sticking by them. Discuss the child's answers to the following questions:

If you get bullied, what should you do?

Tell a responsible adult such as a teacher or parent. If the first person doesn't take any notice, try someone else. You must get adult support.

If an adult makes you uncomfortable in any way, what should you do?

Tell another adult about it. If the first person doesn't listen, tell another, and carry on until you get heard and taken seriously. (All too often, a child's first attempt at telling about something that's happened is ignored and she doesn't try again or not for a very long time. The person may have been busy or distracted and so wasn't paying attention.) You must make the person listen.

(A role-play could be performed where the child wants to tell you that another girl at school hit her, but you are too busy to listen. The child must keep insisting that you stop what you are doing and listen to her. You should eventually reward the child with your full attention, apologise for not realising she had something serious to tell you and praise her for 'sticking with it'.)

If you get blamed for something you didn't do, what should you do?

Try to explain the true situation to the person who has accused you. If he doesn't listen, go to an adult who will and ask him to speak to the person for you.

If you are blamed for something a friend did, ask yourself is it worth it, for the sake of the friendship, to take the blame?

It might be worth it if it was over something small that didn't much matter, but not over anything important. You might lose people's respect because of unfairly taking the blame, or have the wrongdoing on your school record. Your parents might get to hear about it and then it would be far worse still – they would think badly of you.

EXAMPLE

You have tennis lessons with a friend on Saturday mornings. On Sunday afternoon you go to her house and play with her. When her mum sees you, she says, 'It took ages to wash Amita's tennis skirt. She told me you'd pushed her down the bank.' (You didn't and you know nothing about Amita's skirt getting dirty.)

You might be so stunned that you don't know what to say until the moment has passed. If so, ask your friend about it so that she can explain. If Amita gets into enormous trouble for little things, you might decide to take the blame for the sake of your friendship.

Or you might feel very angry that you have been used as a scapegoat and that Amita should take responsibility for what she's done. If she blames you for that, what might she also blame you about in the future? Can you trust her? You could ask her about why she did it and then say, 'Are you going to tell your mum the truth or shall I?'

Or, if you have the presence of mind you could say, 'I don't know what you mean. I didn't push Amita anywhere.'

Knowing what to do and say is sometimes a dilemma. Often you need time to think about it, but by then it may be too late. So, it is a good idea to have a clear picture in your mind as to what behaviour is acceptable to you and what is unacceptable. This makes up your personal rules. Use these to protect yourself.

As you get older, you become more confident about what you expect from friends because you have had more experience of happy times and disappointments.

If someone has been unkind to you, what should you do?

Don't let the person get away with it without bringing it to her attention that you noticed, particularly if she's supposed to be a friend.

EXAMPLE

You have a broken arm and are with a large group of children in the park. One of them, who is a close friend of yours, says, 'Let's run away from Alice.' They all run off, leaving you to follow at a much slower pace as your cast and your sling slow you down.

Tell the person at the next opportunity, preferably when she is on her own, what you think of her behaviour. Say, 'I thought you were my friend. It was not nice of you to get everyone to run away from me. You wouldn't like it if I did it to you!'

Task: Dealing with Put-Downs

Throughout a child's life she will have to cope with people saying things to her with the intention of making her feel bad about herself: these are called put-downs. Using put-downs is a form of bullying. If a child does not protect herself from put-downs, she will be taken advantage of and this will lower her self-esteem. Having the skill to protect herself raises her self-esteem.

To deal assertively with a put-down, a child must not answer back aggressively or passively ignore it, pretending she hasn't heard. (However, she can choose to do this if she feels that's the best way to deal with it; but if she then doesn't tell anyone about it, she risks the same person repeating the experience because he's got away with it. Bullies love people who can't stand up for themselves.)

Examples of put-downs

- Being sarcastic. (Saying, 'Oh, that was clever' when the person drops something.)
- Being rude.

- Calling someone a horrible name.

- Nasty teasing. ('You are a fatty.')

- Implying the person is stupid or silly.

- Giving certain characteristics to all people of the same race. For example, saying all people from a particular country are lazy.

- Having certain expectations because of the sex someone is. For example, expecting all boys to enjoy sports and football and all girls to enjoy dressing up and playing with make-up.

Practice at dealing with put-downs

Discuss with the child what she could say in the following situations. She must try to answer assertively – that is, without using a put-down. She must only respond to what has been said and must not call the person names when replying.

The child might need to respond by splitting up the put-down: to agree with what is true and disagree with anything that is untrue.

1. You are a boy. Friends find out that you are knitting a scarf at home. They laugh and call you a mummy's boy.

    Response: 'I am my mother's son. I'm my father's son too.'

    Or, for older children: 'I'm not restricted by outdated stereotypes. I'm not afraid to be creative in the way I choose.'

    Or: 'I'm not afraid to try out things that you think are girlish. Not doing things like that just because they are girlish is rather an old fashioned way to live.'

2. You did very well in a class test. Your friends are jealous of you and call you a swot.

    Response: 'If you'd learnt the work you'd have done well too. I wouldn't have called you a swot.'

3. Your friends tell you that your clothes aren't any good, that they are cheap and nasty.

Response: *'They are what my parents can afford. It does not change who I am. The way I treat you does not depend on the clothes you wear.'*

Or: *'They are cheap but it's the person inside the clothes that's important.'*

4. You tell your friends that you are getting a brace for your teeth. One of them laughs and says you'll look really strange wearing it.

    Response: *'It may take a while to get used to but I'll have perfect teeth at the end.'*

    Or: *'It won't be for ever and it'll be worth it.'*

5. Someone says you're fat.

    Response: *'I know.'*

    Or: *'Why did you tell me something I already know?'*

Task: Self Put-downs

Sometimes a child might put herself down. This should be discouraged as it will reduce her self-esteem and it points out her weaknesses and failures to others who might take advantage of the knowledge and use it against her.

EXAMPLE

The child tells everyone, 'I'm really stupid because I forgot to bring my homework to school.' This puts ideas into other people's heads. Had she just said 'Oh, I've forgotten my homework', no one might have thought to call her stupid. Forgetful perhaps, but that's not as damaging to her self-esteem.

Write the following headings in the child's file and write her answers to these headings.

What self put-downs do you use?

SUGGESTIONS

- I'm so stupid.
- I'm useless at this sort of thing.
- I hate maths. It's beyond me.
- I'm never any good at crossword puzzles.

What should you say?

SUGGESTIONS

- I wish I'd thought of that.
- I need more practice at this.
- I need extra help with my maths.
- Doing crossword puzzles is not one of my strengths.

What self put-downs do other people use?

SUGGESTIONS

- Oh, I'm not clever like you.
- I could never do anything like that.
- I would never have thought of that.

What do you think of them when they have said those things?

I think it's silly of them to admit it. It makes me feel I have to reassure the person and say, 'Yes you are', 'Yes, you could' or, 'Yes you would'.

Task: Dealing with Criticism

It is not easy for anyone to receive criticism, especially if it is unfair. Any criticism can make a child feel bad about herself, but when the criticism is unfair it is much worse. A child can protect herself from unfair criticism by thinking about what was said very carefully. She should not fight back with an insult but should address exactly what has been said.

Discuss the following examples with the child.

Example 1

Someone tells you that you're mean because you don't lend your friends money. It may be true that you don't, yet children probably shouldn't lend money except in cases of emergency (for example, when someone has lost his bus fare or dinner money). There may be many valid reasons why you don't lend money. You may barely have enough for yourself or you may have been told you aren't allowed to lend money. Or you may have lent it in the past and didn't ever get it back, so decided not to repeat the same mistake.

Response: 'I'm not mean, I wouldn't have enough for my lunch if I lent it. I don't have any spare money with me when I come to school.'

If there is any part of the criticism that you don't agree with, deny it, but be big enough to accept criticism that is true.

Example 2

Your teacher tells you off for being late and calls you lazy as you can't get out of bed in the mornings. You aren't lazy because you do all your homework very carefully and don't mind how long it takes. Your problem is that you go to bed too late and oversleep.

Response: 'I'm sorry I'm late again. It's not that I'm lazy, I go to bed too late and don't get enough sleep.'

Then you will have to be big enough to admit that the situation has to change. It's no good being late and too tired to concentrate in class.

Response: 'I know I'll have to go to bed earlier as I can't keep up the pace. I'll be on time in future.'

Practise at dealing with criticism

Discuss with the child what she could say in the following situations. She must try to answer assertively – that is, without criticising the other person out of revenge. She must only respond to what has been said and must not call the person names when replying.

The child might need to respond by splitting up the criticism: to agree with what is true and disagree with anything that is untrue.

1. Someone tells you that your new hairstyle looks silly. You are proud of it and feel hurt that the person said this.

   Response: 'I'm sorry you don't like it. I'm very pleased with it.'

2. Someone laughs at the way you run when you try to kick the ball.

   Response: 'The game is more important to me than how I look. It's unkind of you to make fun of me.'

3. You come last in a maths test and your friends laugh at you and call you thick.

   Response: 'I do find maths hard but I'm not thick. There are plenty of other subjects I do well in. I see no reason for you to make fun of me.'

4. You're working on a group project and you forgot to do your research over the weekend and have let the group down. They say you're unreliable and have not pulled your weight.

   Response: 'You have every right to be angry with me. But one mistake does not mean I am unreliable or that I'm workshy. I shall do the work tonight and have it ready for tomorrow.'

5. You went to a disco on Saturday night and met someone whom you kissed. All your friends saw you and when you were back in school on Monday they said that you are free and easy and wouldn't care who you kissed as long as you did it.

   Response: 'That's not fair. I met someone I liked and will meet again. I don't go round kissing everyone.'

Task: Giving Criticism

It is hard for people to give criticism assertively – that is, without straying from the point and calling the person names. A child must think what it is about the person's behaviour she doesn't like and then tell the person in such a way as not to cause undue offence.

Discuss the following example with the child.

EXAMPLE

It is no good criticising the fact that someone has told you a lie by saying, 'I hate you!' Instead, you need to challenge the lie.

Response: 'That's not true. Why have you lied to me?'

Here, the person has to concentrate on the fact that she lied and has been caught out, rather than on being told she is hated by you. It makes it much harder for her to wriggle out of her mistake.

Practise at giving criticism

Discuss with the child what she could say in the following situations. She must try to criticise assertively – that is, concentrating on the other person's behaviour: what is wrong with it and perhaps even what the other person could do to improve the situation.

1. Your friend has said that she will not sit by you at lunch if you choose things from the menu she doesn't like.

    Response: 'You can't control what I eat by threatening not to sit by me. If you don't want to sit by me there are plenty of others who will.'

2. Your friend has just invited you to her house but you don't want to go because she always chooses the music you listen to and decides what games to play.

    Response: 'I'm not coming because you don't listen to what I say and you give me no choice over what we do.'

    Or make your own terms: 'Only if we take it in turns to choose what we do and what we listen to. I'm not happy about you choosing every time.'

3. Your mum has some friends round and you overhear her telling them a story about you that is really embarrassing. You feel angry and hurt that she has told other people about it. She should have asked whether you minded.

   Response: 'It was mean of you to tell your friends that story about me. You should have asked if I minded. You'd have been really upset if I'd told my friends something embarrassing you'd done.'

4. You were out with your older brother and did something you weren't allowed to do (but it wasn't dangerous). He told on you the moment you got home. When you and he are on your own you tell him what you thought about it.

   Response: 'I didn't tell on you when you had your friends round and played music so loud the neighbours complained. I feel hurt that you told on me. I don't feel I can trust you again. What I did wasn't that bad and I hadn't put myself in danger.'

5. You are out shopping and a man has just pushed in front of you in the queue.

   Response: 'Excuse me, you've just pushed in. Please take your turn like everyone else.'

   Or: Tell the person serving that he's pushed in so that an adult deals with the situation.

Conclusion

When a child is assertive, she needs to protect herself without losing self-respect and deal with others without making them lose their self-respect. She should always concentrate on the person's behaviour and not make personal comments about the person. This keeps both people focused on the right subject without resorting to name-calling and getting angry and hurt.

As the child learns, and is able to use, assertive skills she will gain confidence and respect from others.

Chapter 9

Handling Feelings

Please note: Anger and anger management are not dealt with in this chapter but in Chapter 10.

It is often difficult for a child to let you know how she feels or to hold back the strength of feeling when she is angry or disappointed. When a child is a toddler, little more may have been expected of her than lying down in the street and screaming because she didn't want to go in a shop, but now that she is older, she needs to learn that this is inappropriate behaviour.

Some feelings are best hidden from the public but can be shown to a caring parent, or another caring adult, while others have every right to make themselves known because of some huge injustice done against the child (such as someone deliberately spoiling her work). It can be difficult for children to know when they are allowed to let rip and when they are not, and what the consequences might be if they display inappropriate feelings.

This chapter explores the different types of feelings children have and helps the child to express them in an appropriate way.

Task: Exploring Feelings

Explain to the child the difference between emotional and physical feelings. (Emotional feelings are how you feel inside your mind, physical feelings are how your body feels.)

Ask the child to name all the emotional and physical feelings she can think of. Write these lists down in her file so that she can consult them when she needs help describing her feelings. It will also help her become accustomed to using a wide variety of descriptions when she communicates how she feels to other people.

If the child cannot think of many feelings, suggest some to her using the lists given below, ensuring she understands what each word means. If necessary, give a sentence to describe the feeling portrayed, using her own experiences and background where possible (the sentences given below are for guidance only and may be inappropriate for all children). You could, for example, ask 'When was the last time you felt angry? Why did you feel angry?' and use her response to create a sentence to go with the feeling word.

Emotional feeling	*Sentence to describe the feeling*
Angry	I felt angry when I found out you'd lied to me.
Anxious	I felt anxious when you weren't where you'd said you'd be.
Bereft	I felt bereft when my best friend moved away.
Bitter	I felt bitter when I saw the present I'd given him kicked under his bed to be forgotten – he never shows pleasure at anything to do with me.
Cheated	I felt cheated when my partner got all the credit for work we'd done together.
Cheerful	I felt cheerful when you told me I could have a friend to tea.
Concerned	I felt concerned when he said he didn't feel well.
Contented	I feel contented when I snuggle up beside you in bed.
Cool	I felt cool towards her when I found out she only pretended to like me because I gave her sweets.
Disappointed	I felt disappointed when you said the tickets had sold out.
Disbelieving	I felt disbelieving when you said everything outside was covered in snow.
Disgusted	I felt disgusted when you described what the butcher did to the chicken.

Distraught	I felt distraught when you said our kitten must be lost somewhere as she'd not been home for over a day and night.
Eager	I felt eager when I knew we were going to buy me a new football T-shirt straight after school.
Embarrassed	I felt so embarrassed when I dropped my ice cream down me because everyone laughed at me.
Empty inside	I felt empty inside when Dad left us.
Exasperated	I felt exasperated having to explain to my baby brother yet again.
Excited	I feel excited at the thought of my birthday tomorrow.
Flustered	I felt flustered when the teacher asked me a question in front of the whole class – I couldn't think straight.
Frantic	I felt frantic when I heard the baby choke. I didn't know what to do.
Frustrated	I feel frustrated when I never seem to be able to do what I want.
Furious	I felt furious when I found out that Matthew had been making up stories about me and spreading rumours.
Glad	I felt glad for Mum when she found out the good news.
Happy	I felt so happy at the fair with my family – we had a great time.
Hard hearted	I felt hard hearted towards him – it's about time I said 'No' and stood up for myself after the way he's taken advantage of me.
Hopeful	As I opened the present I felt so hopeful that it was what I wanted.
Hurt	I felt hurt when you said you didn't love me any more.

Impatient	I felt so impatient waiting for you when I knew we'd probably miss the bus again.
In control	I felt in control when it was me you asked – I thought, I'm the one who can make a difference to what happens.
In love	I felt in love when she turned round and smiled at me.
Interested	I felt interested as soon as you mentioned the word rollerblades.
Irritated	I felt irritated when you apologised for the tenth time – talk about overkill!
Jolly	I felt jolly on the school trip as we all sang on the coach.
Let down	I felt let down when my friend told me he couldn't go with me after all.
Lonely	I felt lonely on my first day at the new school – I didn't know anyone and they all had their friends to talk to.
Mad	I felt mad when you broke my favourite china dog – you were so careless.
Numb	I felt numb when I heard my dog had died – I felt as though I wouldn't ever love a dog again.
Overwhelmed	I felt overwhelmed when you told me how much you cared about me – I didn't know what to say and I was fighting back the tears.
Protective	I felt protective when it was my younger brother's first day at school.
Sad	I felt very sad when Grandma died – I'm going to miss her.
Satisfied	I felt very satisfied when my homework came back with an 'A'.
Scared	I felt scared when I heard the floorboard creak and I knew no one else was supposed to be home.

Shy	I felt shy when I went to the party – I didn't know what to say.
Sorrowful	I felt sorrowful when I thought of all the starving children around the world and wished I could give them some of my food.
Strange	It felt strange calling my mum's new husband 'Dad' – because he wasn't really my dad.
Sympathetic	I felt sympathetic because I knew what it was like – it had happened to me too.
Tearful	I felt tearful when you shouted at me – I don't like it when you get so angry.
Thrilled	I felt thrilled when I knew I'd been picked for the football team.
Uncomfortable	I felt uncomfortable when I was asked to do something I know I'm not allowed to.
Understanding	I felt understanding because it was an easy mistake to make.
Unhappy	I felt unhappy because my friends are all allowed out at the weekends and I'm not.
Upset	I felt upset when I saw the car accident on my way to school.
Weird	I felt weird because I'd not eaten all day – it was horrible.
Worried	I felt worried my mum would find out and tell me off.
Wronged	I felt wronged when Sam told tales about me that weren't true and I got the blame.
Physical feeling	*Sentence to describe the feeling*
Calm	I felt suddenly calm when the moment for my exam came.
Cold	I felt cold when I woke up without any covers over me.

Dizzy	I felt dizzy when I got off the ride at the fair.
Feverish	I felt feverish all afternoon, being very hot one moment and shivering the next – I wasn't surprised I had 'flu.
Frozen	I felt frozen standing in the snow at the bus stop.
Hot	I felt very hot as soon as I stepped out of the shade of the trees.
Hysterical	I felt hysterical when I heard that Mum had been rushed to hospital – I was so frightened about what might happen to her.
Ill	I felt very ill after eating so many sweets.
Jittery	I felt jittery as soon as I was told I had to see the head-teacher.
Numb	My fingers felt numb after the snowball fight.
Restless	I felt restless – I just didn't know what to do and couldn't settle.
Sore	My throat feels sore – I think I must be getting a cold.
Strong	I felt strong after football training.
Tender	The bruise on my leg feels tender to touch.
Tense	My body feels tense – I know I'm worrying.
Tired	I feel tired – I need an early night.
Weak	I feel weak from being in bed for days with 'flu.
Wonderful	I feel wonderful now that I've had a good night's sleep.

Task: Feelings and Friendships

People find it far easier to talk about physical feelings than emotional feelings. For example, some boys may think it's fine to complain about a headache but not to mention that they feel hurt by the way someone spoke to them – it is considered unmanly to worry about the 'finer' emotions.

However, there are many children (and adults) who simply do not know how to talk about the way they feel inside or feel too uncomfortable to admit to these 'weaknesses'. Talking about the way someone feels about something helps others get to know the person and understand him or her better – it's a way of making friends and deepening the relationship. If feelings are never discussed, the relationships can be shallow and unfulfilling.

For example, if a child has never told anyone about the emotional turmoil she is suffering, she won't find it easier when the problem worsens or hits crisis point. She also won't know who would respond best with the information and who could be trusted and who couldn't. We often 'test the water' with small confidences about the way we feel before giving more valuable information to someone, after the person has proved he or she can be trusted.

Discuss the following questions with the child:

How do you get to know someone well?

- By listening to what he or she has to say.

- By encouraging the person to show his or her feelings and not being embarrassed when the person does.

- By being around when something bad or good happens to the person.

What should you do when someone tells you about the way she feels?

- Be interested – if she has brought up the subject, she is prepared to talk about it. Ask her to explain what has been happening to make her feel this way.

- Be sympathetic – if you laugh or brush off her fears she is more likely to clam up and not trust you again to deal sensitively with her problems.

- Show that you understand how she feels or, if you don't, ask her to explain in more depth to help you understand.

- Offer support, such as suggesting ways around her problem (this is not the same as telling her what to do – it is just giving her ideas that she might not have thought of herself). Or, if you can't see a way round, be there for her as she lives through the problem, giving a sympathetic ear so that she can regularly update you on how things are and get comfort from sharing her problem.

How can the friendship be further deepened?

If the confidence-telling is all one-way, there is an imbalance in the friendship. This is fine for a short while, while someone is in a crisis, but if it were to continue long term, it might affect the closeness of your relationship. This person has put her trust in you and will feel hurt if you don't put yours in her. If you never tell about the things that are close to your heart, she will feel pushed away and the friendship may never progress further. Very good friends support one another and listen to one another – it is a two-way process.

Task: Describing Feelings

Discuss the following situations with the child and ask her to think how she would feel. This helps her think about her emotions and learn to verbalise them. Many people lack this very important social skill. They find it hard or impossible to talk about their feelings and bottle things up inside themselves. In doing this, they are preventing others from getting to know them better and are distancing themselves from any possible emotional support, making it more likely that they become lonely. They are also more likely to react to strong emotions in an inappropriate way. For example, they might become very aggressive if angry rather than discussing the problem calmly.

Situation 1

Your baby brother smashes your work of art with his wooden hammer and then laughs at you when he sees your face. How do you feel?
(Angry, disappointed, frustrated, hurt.)

Situation 2

You watch a puppy being operated on in the television programme *Animal Hospital* and they say he might die.
(Disgusted or interested (at the blood and the puppy's insides being shown), hopeful, sad, scared, tense, worried.)

Situation 3

You are being accused of taking a bar of chocolate out of a shop without paying for it – but you had paid.
(Angry, bitter, frustrated, scared, wronged.)

Task: Controlling Your Feelings

Here we shall look at situations where the child should keep a rein on her feelings. Discuss the situations with her and ask her what she should do.

Situation 1

Someone asks you to hand over your dinner money (in cash) or he'll hit you. He's bigger than you, and you feel very frightened. What should you do?

(Give him the money to get away from him and then tell a teacher what he's done or, if it happens out of school, tell your parents. Don't show that you're terribly frightened, as that would make him more pleased with himself. If he thinks you are not as frightened as he would like, he may not bother to bully you again.)

Situation 2

Your friends decide to ignore you and leave you out for some reason. You feel like crying. What should you do?

(Pretend you don't care and carry on as though nothing out of the ordinary has happened. They are doing this to hurt your feelings, so try not to let them know they've succeeded. Tell your parents about it when you get home.)

Situation 3

Your older sister is winding you up. She knows all the buttons to press (how to get to you) and you are furious with her. What should you do?

(Don't hit out or hurt her. The best thing would be to walk away. The sooner she knows that she can't play those sorts of games with you any more, the sooner she will stop trying. It will be too boring for her to keep on if you don't rise in anger.)

Task: Letting Feelings Out

Sometimes it is good for a child to let others know how she feels. If someone has hurt her feelings, they should know that they've done wrong and be given the opportunity to apologise. Also, if a child bottles up all her feelings she will have difficulty coping with the frustration. The difficult thing is to know when to keep them in check and when to let them out for all to see. The following situations involve needing to let out feelings. Discuss these with the child and talk about how she might express her feelings.

Situation 1

You were told that you could go away on the school trip to an outdoor pursuits centre. At the last minute your parents changed their minds and said you couldn't go.

    (a) How would you feel?

    (b) How would you show these feelings?

    (c) What might happen if you don't show these feelings?

SUGGESTIONS

    (a) I would feel angry, disappointed, disbelieving, cheated, let down.

    (b) I would show these feelings by crying; shouting 'It's not fair!'; asking for an explanation; stamping my foot or walking out and slamming the door.

    (c) If my parents know that they shouldn't have let my hopes be dashed without warning they may accept most, if not all, of this (negative) behaviour. But what they probably won't accept is any name-calling. If I don't show these feelings, my parents will think that I wasn't that bothered about going anyway and so will not rethink what they've done for now or the future.

Situation 2

Your best friend is emigrating to another country and you don't know whether you'll ever see her again. The moment comes when you say goodbye.

(a) How would you feel?

(b) How would you show these feelings?

(c) What might happen if you don't show these feelings?

SUGGESTIONS

(a) I would feel bereft, distraught, sad, tearful, unhappy.

(b) I would show these feelings by crying and hugging her tight or kissing her; making promises about keeping in touch, unable to think that I will completely have to let go; exchanging special gifts to remind us of each other; taking her photo.

(c) If I do not show these feelings, my friend will think I don't care about her. She may also wonder what the friendship meant to me when we were together.

Situation 3

You've recently met a very funny boy. The jokes he tells makes you want to double up with laughter. Think about when you are with him.

(a) How would you feel?

(b) How would you show these feelings?

(c) What might happen if you don't show these feelings?

SUGGESTIONS

(a) I would feel very happy and jolly.

(b) I would show these feelings by laughing openly, without trying to smother it; telling him he's very funny; showing I enjoy being with him by asking him about his plans for his free time and suggesting we spend some of it together.

(c) By showing these feelings I am rewarding him for his behaviour – I am telling him that he makes me feel good and that will make him feel good. Trying to hide my enjoyment of his company is likely to make him want to steer clear of mine.

Task: Showing Your Gentler Feelings

It can be very hard for some people to show the gentler side to their nature. This can be particularly true of boys because of the way they have been brought up ('to be a man') and because of the way society expects men and boys to behave (not to show weaknesses and to be always strong and in control). However, all children need help in expressing themselves and in giving sympathy and love to others because it means they are showing the more vulnerable inner part of themselves, which will make others warm to them.

Discuss the following situations with the child to see how she would express her gentler feelings.

Situation 1

Your friend is diabetic. One day, at the end of a lesson, you notice your friend standing by the window looking out onto the playground. You ask him if he's going to join you but he makes no reply. Going closer, you realise there's something wrong. When you touch his arm you find it stiff and unyielding. You shout to the teacher for help and with others, you lower your friend onto some desks. He is unconscious. You wait with him while the teacher 'phones for an ambulance. How would you feel and how would you express these feelings?

SUGGESTIONS

I would feel worried and concerned. I would feel hurt for him and would feel the need to comfort him, although I know he would not know anything about it.

I would express these feelings by touching him, holding his hand, stroking his brow, running my fingers through his hair, talking softly and encouragingly to him, telling him not to worry and that help was on its way. I would cover his body with my coat to keep him warm. I would cushion his head with my jumper.

Situation 2

Your best friend has school phobia. You know that he finds the first hour of school horrendous. His body shakes, he feels ill, he's sometimes sick and he finds it hard to concentrate. How would you feel and how would you express these feelings?

SUGGESTIONS

I would feel brotherly/sisterly/fatherly/motherly towards him, concerned, protective, sorry for him, sympathetic, understanding.

I would express these feelings by meeting him when he arrives in school and looking after him: being close by and being friendly towards him, expecting nothing in return by way of response and looking after him when he's being sick: getting him water to drink afterwards. When he's not in a panic, I would ask him what he's thinking and why he finds coming to school so awful. I would stop others from making fun; I would make the lessons as easy as possible by patiently explaining what we need to do; I would help him find his PE kit or anything else so that he has as little to worry about as possible. I would be kind to him and share my sweets.

Task: Shyness

A child not only needs opportunities to mix with other children but also to have the chance to relate to people of all ages and to people in authority (such as her teacher, karate instructor, friends' parents and religious leader) to become socially multi-skilled. The more practice a child gets at communicating successfully with others, the better she will be able to cope when she later relies on others for being given a job and for working in a team.

There is also one other, very important reason why a child should overcome her feelings of shyness. They can act as a barrier between a child and her relationships. If, for example, a child is so overcome with shyness that she cannot hold a conversation with another person whom she does not know well, she is cutting herself off from all new relationships. She is so taken up with how awkward she is feeling that she cannot show interest in another person or his or her life. This does not bode well for forming close relationships. A child needs to be sufficiently content with herself and confident about her abilities to let go and stop thinking of how uncomfortable she is feeling. She should learn to put those feelings aside and concentrate on the more positive aspects of talking to others.

Discuss the following questions with the child. Then discuss any suggested answers that the child had not thought of herself.

Why are people shy?

- They feel uncomfortable in other people's presence.

- They are too aware of themselves to think of being interested in the other person.

- They are not aware that other people can be fascinating once you get them talking.

- They can't be bothered to make the effort to talk and be friendly.

Why are you shy? Why do you think that is?

When are you shy?

- When I meet people I don't know very well or haven't spent a great deal of time with.
- When I'm among adults. (I feel so small and can't think of what to say.)
- When I have to do something in front of the class or in assembly.

When are you not shy?

- When I'm with my friends.
- When I'm with my family.
- When I'm on my own.

What do you get out of being shy?

- I don't have to make too much effort thinking up things to say.
- It's a good excuse when I don't want to talk to someone.
- I never get asked to do things because I don't look confident enough to cope.
- I can blend into the background and not be noticed.

What do you get out of being friendly and chatty to someone?

- I make more friends.
- My friendships can be deeper because I take the trouble to get to know someone really well.
- I feel good because when I'm interested in someone, they are generally interested in me too.
- I get to know much more about life since so many interesting things happen to other people.

- I can exchange knowledge and experiences – this makes me a more wise and understanding person.

- I never know what I might be missing out on if I don't bother to find out about the person inside the body facing me.

- It is good practice for when someone extremely interesting comes along or for when I'm in a tricky job situation – I will handle events more smoothly.

How would you like people to think of you?

Would you like someone to think that you're rude or lazy because you can't be bothered to talk to him or her or would you like someone to admire you for the effort you put in to being polite and friendly? More importantly, how would you like to see yourself? As a blushing wall-flower or a confident and assertive individual with thoughts and opinions you are ready to share with others?

Task: Shyness Action Plan

Ask the child to think up things to do to reduce her shyness. Write them down in her file, putting the easiest things first and ending with the hardest. Then, over the next few weeks, set her these tasks and tick them off when she has done them. Some may be done more than once: the more ticks the better. The more she practises, the easier it becomes.

Suggestions

- Say 'Hello' to another school-aged child whom I regularly see on my way to or from school.

- Smile and say 'Hello' to my friends when I see them for the first time each day.

- Smile at people in my school that I know by sight as I walk past them.

- Ask a teacher a question at the end of the lesson.
- Put my hand up in class to answer a question.
- Ask the teacher a question in class, in front of the other pupils.
- Talk to pupils from other classes.
- Offer to take a message to another teacher.
- Offer to help carry equipment or books for a teacher.
- If someone falls over in the playground, ask the person if he or she is all right.
- Speak to my neighbours (with my parents' permission).
- Offer to help an old person with his or her shopping.
- Contribute more to the conversations I have with my friends.
- Accept invitations to go out with friends or to a party or disco.
- Invite friends to my house (with my parents' permission).

Task: Role-Plays: Overcoming Shyness

Role-play 1

Pretend that you are a new boy or girl at the child's school and she has been given the responsibility of looking after you. She must take you on a (pretend) tour of the school explaining about break-times and lunchtime and how you have to queue. Since you are so shy, the child must make all the effort of talking and should try to get to know you better. (Ideally, she should be sufficiently skilled to make it a balanced conversation so that if you tell her how old you are, she should say how old she is without being asked.)

If the child has a younger brother or sister, she might be skilled at this role-play because of being used to explaining things to another child. In this case, you could try an alternative: the child being responsible for showing a new teacher (you) around the school. She must answer the teacher's questions as fully as possible, without resorting to yes/no answers.

THINGS TO OBSERVE IN ROLE-PLAY 1

- Did the child speak loudly enough for you to hear?
- Did the child look you in the eyes when she spoke to you?
- Did she explain things fully or just say 'There's the dining hall' without explaining what you have to do to get lunch and what time it is?
- Was her speech fluent or were there many stops and starts with uncomfortable silences in between?
- Did she give you any advice about the school? (Such as which teachers were kind or strict, things you really mustn't do or which lunches were yuck?)
- Did the child invite you to ask her questions?

Role-play 2

You are the shopkeeper and the child wants to look at (and then buy) a toy or game that is too high up for her to reach. She must come to you, explain what she wants and then go through the motions of looking at it, buying it and waiting for change.

After the role-play, ask the child to analyse the situation, suggesting what bits went well and which needed to be improved upon.

THINGS TO OBSERVE IN ROLE-PLAY 2

- Did the child say 'Excuse me?' to grab your attention?
- Did she clearly explain what she wanted and then politely ask if you could get the toy down for her?
- Did she tell you she would buy it or did she just stand there until you prompted her?
- Did the child smile at you as she handed over the money?

- Did the child make eye contact with you when she talked or listened to you?
- Did she thank you when you handed her the toy?
- Did she say 'Goodbye'?

Constant revision of social expectations improves a child's performance. The praise you give her will fuel her motivation and her shyness will recede. It doesn't matter if it is still evident – that may be part of her personality. The important thing is that it does not become a handicap. A child's shyness should not rule her life, she should rule it.

Parental Pages on Shyness

Photocopiable for professional use within the institution that bought the book, to use to help parents reduce their child's shyness.

Task: Parents: Shyness and Self-Confidence

This task is for parents to do with their child.

Your child will have difficulty eliminating shyness if she is low on self-confidence. Remind her of all the positive qualities and special talents she has and boost her self-esteem by complimenting her whenever the situation merits it.

Action plan for parents to boost their child's confidence in social situations

- Warn your child beforehand what to expect from the situation.

- Explain how you would like, or expect, her to behave.

- Tell her you might give gentle (unobtrusive) reminders or hints at appropriate times and that she should understand straight away what you mean by them. (Practise beforehand.) For example, you could tell her that if you squeeze her elbow it's to remind her to look someone in the eye and say 'Hello', 'Goodbye' or 'Thank you for having me'.

- Remind your child of things she should not say or do.

- Praise your child for any positive social move she makes when you are in private and tell her how proud of her you are.

- Ask your child to think of things she might have forgotten to do.

- Ask your child to think of things she could have done to make the situation even better.

- Ask your child if she spotted anyone make a social mistake. Then ask what the person ought to have done.

Carry out the above steps with your child for even the simplest of social occasions.

Conclusion

The feelings that a child has are part of what makes her special. By telling people how she feels she keeps in touch with herself and allows others to get to know her better. The more she practises verbalising her feelings, the more skilled she will become at understanding her behaviour and saying what is troubling her rather than taking out her frustration in a physical way. Keeping in touch with her feelings will also help her understand other people and the reasons for some of their negative behaviour.

It is unreasonable to expect a child to mention feelings frequently if no one else at home does. Explain to the child's parents that they should try to share the ups and downs of the day so that their child becomes used to 'feeling talk'.

Being able to express feelings is an important safety valve that, if not used, may lead to depression later on: in teenage years or in adult life. People can feel cut off from others and may feel there is no one to turn to in times of trouble. This is particularly true for boys as they are not traditionally encouraged to talk about feelings and tend to have less emotionally supportive relationships than girls.

Chapter 10

Anger

Anger is a very powerful emotion which, if uncontrolled, can cause great damage. It is often accompanied by feelings of depression, frustration, hurt, jealousy, low self-esteem, self-hatred and worry. Anger drives people to aggression and can manifest itself in verbal abuse, physical abuse, self-harm and vandalism.

If the anger is 'chronic', it may be more general, where the child sees little good in anything or anyone, and is forever criticising, putting people down, being sarcastic, being cynical, and making snide comments behind someone's back. The child may also be irritable and 'on a short fuse' where the slightest incident can spark off a chain reaction of unleashed fury. The temporary release of fury and pent-up frustration from within might be satisfying at the time, but the child must pay for the consequences afterwards.

This chapter is concerned with understanding anger and learning to use it positively instead of negatively, which is when relationships, people or objects get hurt.

Task: Understanding Anger

This task is about discussing angry behaviour and understanding its repercussions or consequences. Ask the child to give examples of different angry acts in the categories given, and to answer the questions following about behaviour.

Verbal abuse

- Swearing.
- Name-calling.
- Shouting or screaming (can include throwing a tantrum).
- Sarcasm.
- Putting down.

Physical abuse

- Hitting.
- Kicking.
- Punching.
- Hair-pulling.
- Arm-twisting.
- Biting.
- Scratching.
- Pulling to the ground.

What are the consequences of doing the above things?

- They create aggression in the other person (unless that person is too timid to fight back – in which case, are you bullying and taking advantage of the person's gentler nature?).
- You would probably be 'sworn enemies' with each other. Your behaviour would have built up hatred on both sides. It would not be easy to be friends again with the other person.
- The aggression, on both sides, might spiral out of control and you would have a situation that could not be easily repaired, and a situation that could result in serious injury or even death.

Self-harm

- Cutting yourself.
- Knocking your head against a wall.

- Biting yourself.
- Starving yourself.
- Overeating.
- Over-drinking.
- Taking illegal drugs.
- Solvent-sniffing.
- Stealing.
- Isolating yourself and withdrawing from social contact.
- Punishing yourself in any other way.

What are the consequences of self-harm?

- You hurt yourself physically.
- You hurt yourself psychologically (or emotionally). It lowers your self-esteem to damage your body by not taking care of it or by deliberately hurting it.
- You may become depressed.
- You may become addicted (to substances or to damaging eating patterns).
- You may become lonely.
- You may lose your friends.

Vandalism

- Smashing things.
- Kicking things.
- Pulling things off the wall.
- Tearing or ripping things up.
- Setting fire to things.
- Ripping electrical equipment from wall sockets.
- Spray-painting buildings.
- Urinating (weeing), or defecating (pooing), in inappropriate places.

What are the consequences of vandalism?

- You may damage something you, or someone close to you, values.
- You may damage your body doing it.
- You may be made to buy replacements or pay for repairs or cleaning.
- You may be arrested if you damage public property.
- You may end up with a police record.
- You do not learn to respect other people's property or the public's right to have certain services (such as the use of a public telephone).

What do you get from using any of the above angry behaviour (negative and positive things)?

POSITIVE THINGS

- You relieve your frustration.
- You let your anger 'burn out'.
- It is a way of showing people that you are hurting inside.

NEGATIVE THINGS

- You have increased your aggression.
- You have increased the other person's aggression.
- You have made a fool of yourself – letting people see you out of control.
- You have produced a situation of conflict.
- You have built a wall of hatred between you and another person.
- You would not have got your argument across – you were too busy abusing the person.
- You would have produced a situation that is not easy to repair.

- You would have lost a friend (or potential friend). Or you may have damaged the relationship you have with someone such as your parents or someone else who has a long term role in your life.

- With self-harm, you have harmed yourself. You may need medical attention. It severely damages your self-esteem when you turn your anger in on yourself, and you may need professional help.

- With vandalism, you might be arrested, or made to pay for the damage you have done. You might have broken something irreplaceable and hurt the owner's feelings (it might be yours).

- It does not solve the original problem.

Most of the negative consequences are long-lived – you will have to deal with them long after the situation has passed. So, for just a short burst of uncontrolled anger, you have brought much trouble on yourself.

When is anger a positive emotion?

- It lets you know that there's something wrong and you need to do something about it.

- It fires you up for making a positive change in your life, or for taking positive action such as making a complaint.

- It shows that there is something amiss within a relationship and can show a friend, or partner, that a problem needs to be discussed. It can then spark off new ground rules for a better relationship.

- It can get rid of the bad feelings you have – such as when you scream and hit a pillow to take out your frustration – without damaging anyone. Afterwards, you may feel calm and better able to think clearly about what needs to be done to improve things.

However, for anger to have positive consequences, you need to use it in a channelled way so that it works *for* you, not against you.

Task: Angry People

Sometimes anger is absolutely understandable and justifiable. In such cases, it is not a problem unless it gets out of control and someone gets physically hurt. This is a 'normal' use of anger. But some people are in a state of aggression where the slightest thing can push them into a very angry mood, one that is totally out of proportion to the event that caused it.

Discuss with the child why some people are 'angry people'. Write her suggestions in her file.

Suggestions why some people are 'angry people'
(There may be several factors that work together to build up a person's anger.)

- They have had many things go wrong in their life and life has been tough for them.

- They have often been hurt and they feel like lashing out at others, wanting others to suffer too.

- They live with angry people and so have learnt to act in an aggressive way.

- They see someone react violently to something that later happens to themselves – and they then feel the pent-up anger and frustration of this other person and react in the same way. (A good example of this is a person using exactly the same angry words as his parent has used with him. Memories like this can survive a long time without conscious knowledge and suddenly, in reaction to an event, the words can come spilling out as though the parent were speaking through that person.)

- They have a low self-esteem and get more easily upset about things than a happy, confident person would. They might be aggressive to cover up their hurt and bad feelings about themselves.

- They feel frustrated that they can't get, or do, something they really want.

- They feel unable to control events around them. (They feel powerless in their own life so go to great lengths to have an effect over something else.)

- They bottle up their feelings until they 'explode' – a small event that someone else might not think anything of may trigger an enormous reaction because it is, for the person, the 'last straw'.

- They feel unable to cope with something that has happened, or is happening, to them such as their parents splitting up or divorcing, becoming chronically sick or breaking up with a best friend.

- They have a big disappointment that they can't handle, such as something previously promised to them being later denied.

- They are not good at sharing their problems or their feelings with someone else.

- They have no one else to share their problems and feelings with.

- They have been pushed beyond what they can stand such as being abused, bullied or over-pressurised and they take out their emotional pain on others they see as weaker than themselves, or on themselves.

Task: Your Anger

The form that anger takes has been looked at; now the child's own experience of anger will be examined. Ask the following questions for one big occasion when the child was angry. Write the questions with her responses in her file. Her answers are important, as they will be used again later, in 'Task: Parents: Role-Play: Practise at Managing Your Anger'.

What made you angry?

What did you do?

What were the consequences?

Was it worth while to be angry in the way you were? (Did something positive come out of it?)

What have you learnt about your angry behaviour (generally)?

SUGGESTIONS

- It doesn't always get me what I want.
- I feel bad afterwards because I don't like myself for what I have done and fear others won't like me either.
- After the event I feel ashamed of the way I behaved and feel embarrassed that others have seen my behaviour.
- I am losing friends because of it.
- My life at home is harder because of it – my parents have lost patience with me and my siblings (brothers and sisters) have shut me out of their lives.
- I've got a name for myself – people now expect me to 'fly off the handle'.
- People avoid me because they think I'm trouble.

Parental Pages on Anger

Photocopiable for professional use within the institution that bought the book, to use to help parents help their child with anger management.

Although these pages have been written as though talking to the child herself, they should be read by an adult (parent or professional) and then explained to the child at a level appropriate to her age and understanding. If the child is able, however, to make use of them as they stand, the adult should read through the pages with her and discuss the suggestions, and how the parent *and* child could make use of them when interacting with each other.

There is too much information to take in at one go – the pages should be repeatedly read and discussed over a period of time to gradually shift aggressive behaviour to a more positively channelled one. They may be used to discuss an angry argument that has occurred, to see where things went awry and how the issues could have been better dealt with.

Things you can do to bring your anger under control

CALM YOURSELF

- Count to 10 or 20, forwards or backwards, to stop your immediate response of lashing out in some way.

- Briefly hold your breath or gently bite your lip or tongue to stop you from blurting out something you may later regret. Try to focus on your heartbeat to get it back to normal. (When you are angry, your heart starts to race.)

- Try to stop all the 'angry' hormones being produced. Try to think calmly about the problem instead of how angry you feel. You will feel better and less enraged if you do this.

- Learn to relax. Be aware of the tension in your muscles and deliberately try to relax them. If anger is a big problem for you, seek professional help and learn relaxation techniques. (This involves muscle clenching and relaxing, deep breathing from the diaphragm and relaxing imagery. It is also possible to buy relaxation audio tapes from book shops.)

TALK TO YOURSELF

Replace angry thoughts with 'self-talk' that soothes.

Tell yourself:

- 'Anyone would feel like this if they'd had it done to them.'
- 'I can beat this anger thing and keep control.'
- 'These awful feelings of rage will pass.'
- 'It will help me to talk to someone about what's happened and how I feel.'
- 'I'm tired, I'm probably overreacting.'
- 'I've had a bad day. I mustn't take that out on someone else now. It had nothing to do with him or her.'
- 'If I lose control, I won't get anywhere – I know because I've tried it that way before.'
- 'I know that I must concentrate on the problem, not how I feel.'

Ask yourself:

- 'Does it really matter?'
- 'Am I being unreasonable?'
- 'Am I being fair?'
- 'Should I accept some responsibility for what has happened?'
- 'Am I being honest with myself?'

LEARN TO LET GO

- Not everything is worth the fuss of getting angry about. Recognise those times where you can just let the matter drop and ignore what has been said or done. Teach yourself to react to only things that matter to you.

- Some people deliberately taunt because they know they can get a reaction. Don't fall into the trap of allowing yourself to be played like a puppet.

- Rethink your personal rules – you do not have to take out revenge on everyone that does, or says, something to upset you. Life is not about having a personal crusade against everyone that has 'done you wrong'.

- Try to laugh off the lesser irritating things that someone does, or says, to you. See pettiness for what it is and don't react violently.

SUPPRESS YOUR VIOLENT AND AGGRESSIVE FEELINGS

Try to damp down what you are feeling so that your aggression does not get out of control. This helps you focus more on the problem than on how your heart is racing and the fact that your muscles are tensed for action.

This can be especially hard if you are going through an emotional time yourself such as puberty, or if you have had a great disappointment, have trouble at home, or are suffering bereavement. Whatever it is that is adding pressure in your life, try to recognise it. Such strains put your emotions higher up on the anger scale to begin with, so that any additional annoyance makes your anger peak in no time at all and for very little reason.

Be understanding of yourself. Keep in touch with your own emotions and try to explain these emotions to the people who are important in your life. Don't be too hard on yourself.

AVOID UNNECESSARY CONFLICT

- Don't use accusing language. (Usually this means any sentence starting with the word 'you'.) For example, 'You shouldn't have done that', 'You said you'd do it', 'You lied to me.' Instead you could say 'Why did you do that?', 'I thought it would have been done by now', and, 'I don't like being lied to.'

- Find out the reasons why something has happened, before accusing.

- Give the person a chance to explain.

- Lower your expectations of outcome – you don't have to have it entirely your way. Half your way and half his or hers would do.

- Accept that people make mistakes without doing it on purpose.
- Accept that there isn't always an answer to every problem.
- Don't say the first thing that comes into your head. When feelings are on edge, you need to tread carefully. You are more likely to get what you want if you do.
- Take your time responding to what the other person says.
- Accept that the other person has needs, just like you.

SEE PEOPLE AS PEOPLE

- Get to know the people around you.
- Notice their positive points.
- Notice their weak points.
- Don't look at a person over-critically – no one is perfect. Try to see the person as a person rather than an enemy or someone to be despised. Is there a reason why the person behaves like he or she does? Does that make the person's behaviour more understandable?
- Check you don't have prejudices against any particular group of people. Prejudices aren't true – you'd be giving yourself unnecessary grief over nothing. You would also be stirring up dislike and hatred for no reason. Try to find differences between people interesting instead of comparing them negatively with yourself.
- If someone has offended you, do you blame him or her for one mistake for ever more?
- Try to be more tolerant. Give people more chances.
- Try to be forgiving of others – practise forgiving yourself too; it will make you less angry because you will feel more satisfied with yourself.

TRY TO DEAL WITH THE PROBLEM PRODUCTIVELY (IN A POSITIVE WAY)

- Focus on the problem.

- Ignore personal comments for the time being and home in on the issue that has caused the problem.

- Talk to the person who has upset you. Explain your point of view.

- Explain what you think is the other person's point of view – it shows you have understood his or her side and it encourages the other person to co-operate.

- Don't interrupt the other person. Wait until it is your turn to speak and then get your point across.

- Don't hog the conversation.

- Show the other person you are willing to be reasonable and suggest a compromise.

- If you are both too angry to talk at the time, suggest meeting up later to discuss the problem, when you have both had a chance to think about it logically (sensibly).

- If you cannot come to an agreement, try again another time when you have both had longer to think about the situation.

- If you are criticised, don't fight back with a knee-jerk reaction. Ask yourself if there is any truth to the criticism – and be honest. Then think carefully how to respond.

- If you are in any part to blame, admit it – that immediately defuses the situation. You need not accept blame for everything. If you accept part of the blame, the other person is encouraged to admit to the other part.

Remind yourself of all the reasons why anger is unhelpful – look at your file and remember the consequences of your uncontrolled anger.

Task: Parents: Role-Play: Practise at Managing Your Anger

This task is for parents to do with the help of the professional. It is important for parents to understand how to respond positively to their child when she is making an effort to curb her anger.

For those children that already have quick, hot temperaments, it is vital that they understand the importance of channelling their anger into something positive, so that a step forward has been made, or a greater level of understanding reached. It is a waste of energy for it to be otherwise.

Pick the occasion when your child was angry from 'Task: Your Anger' to work on. You will take on the role of the person who did the thing that made your child angry. Your child must think of alternative, positive, ways to deal with her anger which you can discuss with her first, before the role-play. Once your child is clear about how she can behave positively, act out the scene as a role-play. (Read through the entire example first and discuss it with your child so that she and you understand what you are aiming for. Then use it as a framework for your pre-role-play discussion.)

Example

You had been looking forward to a friend being invited round at the weekend. Your parents had promised that, because you had been so co-operative lately, they'd invite a friend of your choice to tea. But when Saturday came, you were told that you couldn't have the friend round after all because your mum had forgotten that you needed to be taken to get new trainers for school. There was no other convenient time to invite the friend that weekend.

The following headings are from 'Task: Your Anger':

WHAT MADE YOU ANGRY?

My mum had promised my friend could come round but she changed her mind.

WHAT DID YOU DO?

- I screamed at her and told her that it wasn't fair, she'd broken her promise.
- I told her I wasn't going to keep my promises either.
- I told her to stuff the new trainers, I didn't want them.
- I called her a liar – I told her she hadn't meant to invite my friend in the first place.

WHAT WERE THE CONSEQUENCES?

- She got angry with me and told me I was ungrateful.
- She said I didn't deserve new trainers but I had to have them because the others had fallen apart.
- She told me to go to my room and get out of her sight.
- She said she'd tell Dad how I behaved as soon as he got home.

WAS IT WORTH WHILE TO BE ANGRY IN THE WAY YOU WERE? (DID SOMETHING POSITIVE COME OUT OF IT?)

- We both felt bad.
- I stayed angry and so did Mum.
- I got pulled round the shops and Mum hardly spoke to me.
- I got into more trouble when Dad got home.

No, it wasn't worth it. Nothing positive came out of it.

Preparation for this task

WHAT COULD YOU HAVE DONE?

- Held my breath for a short while to stop me from speaking.
- Counted from ten down to zero.
- Shown the disappointment on my face.

WHAT COULD YOU HAVE SAID?

- 'I feel really angry and disappointed.'
- 'I was really looking forward to my friend coming.'
- 'I don't feel like going shopping. I feel grumpy and angry with you.'
- 'When can my friend come then?'

WHAT WOULD BE THE CONSEQUENCES?

- My mum would be more prepared to listen to my point of view.
- She would offer sympathy and say that she understood I was disappointed.
- She would apologise for having to change the plan.
- She would suggest another time my friend could come.
- She might try to comfort me by hugging me.
- She might give me a treat when we are out to help make up for it.

WOULD IT BE WORTH WHILE TO MAKE THE EFFORT TO KEEP MY ANGER IN CHECK?

Yes, if the consequences mentioned above happened.

Note for parents

It is important that you are aware of what the anger management task involves, because you must be prepared to meet your child halfway. You must be equally prepared to say sorry and offer a compromise and you must make every effort to reward your child when she is trying to keep her anger under control. If your child does not find managing her anger a rewarding experience, she will stop trying.

Try to understand when your child is sorely disappointed. Can you remember any time from your childhood when your parents did not understand your feelings? How did that make you feel? How did you react towards them?

It often isn't your child you react to when she has done something wrong, but events that happened in your own childhood, and in your role as parent you may feel your own parents' anger spill out of you.

Volatile parents react in similar ways to their angry child (certainly the parent in the example given above does). So, it is vital that you yourselves fully understand how to try to curb your anger, to provide ground for your child to try out her new techniques. If she is quashed at every attempt, she will not get past the start. With both 'sides' learning to control how their anger manifests itself, a better, more trusting relationship might ensue where both 'sides' enjoy each other's company all the more.

IF YOUR PARENTS WERE TRYING TO MANAGE THEIR ANGER TOO, HOW SHOULD THEY REACT?

- Listen to me.

- Sympathise with me.

- Say sorry.

- Give another time when they will invite my friend.

- Comfort me through my disappointment.

- Give me a treat to try to lessen the disappointment.

- *Say how proud they are of me for understanding.*

- *Say how proud they are of me for not throwing a wobbly.*
- *Reassure me, saying how much they love me.*

The last three points above are essential for making your child feel good about herself, proud that she has done well and eager to repeat the positive experience. She will also feel loved and this will further boost her self-esteem. Your child has still had the same disappointment – but the way it has been handled on both sides bears no comparison to the outbursts of rage and dissatisfaction.

Returning to your child's task, ask the questions outlined in the above example to provide a framework on which to work. Then act the scene with your child with both sides meeting each other halfway.

After the role-play, discuss how it went. How did your child feel? Could she have responded to you (or whoever had upset her) in this way? If not, why not? Is it something that could be worked on?

Homework

Your child, with your knowledge, must try to work on her anger. She should tell you how she feels when something doesn't go according to plan – and you must be prepared to listen. You should also confide your feelings to your child so that she gets to understand you better too.

Conclusion

Anger management is essentially about improving communication with oneself as well as with others, understanding one's own and other people's needs and commiserating with oneself and with others when these are not met. It is also about finding alternative solutions and working with others (not against them) for a common aim – that of a more harmonious, 'equal' relationship. (Here, equal refers to each having a right to express their feelings and opinions in a positive way; it has nothing to do with children making all their own decisions about what they do or how they should behave – they are still in much need of instructed guidance.)

Another important aspect of anger management is that of being able to forgive: people's weaknesses, their failings and their past mistakes. It is also vital to forgive oneself and see oneself as a loveable person.

Chapter 11

Social Situations

By now, the child will have learnt about the rules that go with different social settings such as how to behave in the swimming pool, at the cinema or in school. All of these settings have rules attached to them. So do situations.

Task: Role-Play: Greetings

A situation is described under each heading. Ask the child to think about what is expected of her behaviour when she is in that particular situation. Then act it out. She needs to be as socially skilled as possible.

Arriving at a friend's house

Your friend's mother opens the door. She has her apron on and you can smell something baking. How should you greet her?

SUGGESTION

Smile widely and look pleased to see her. Then say, 'Hello Mrs X. What a wonderful smell. Have you been baking?' This opens up the conversation so that she is invited to tell you what she has made. It makes your arrival more fluid without stiff exchanges of greeting and you disappearing as quickly as you can to your friend's room. Note that you must call your friends' parents by their formal names unless they have given you permission to call them by their first names.

Leaving a friend's house

You are going home after having had tea. You and your friend are in the hall and his parents are sitting in the lounge watching television.

SUGGESTION

Say, 'Thanks, I had a great time. Can I go and say goodbye to your parents?' Then do it and thank them for having you round and for the meal. It is not nice for anyone's parents to feel they are taken for granted and they will be very pleased if you make an effort to thank them. It will also mean they will be happy for you to continue coming round.

Task: Rules for Greetings

Using the above role-plays for ideas, ask the child to think up a list of general rules for when people say 'Hello' to someone and when people say 'Goodbye'. Write them down in the child's file.

SUGGESTIONS OF RULES FOR SAYING 'HELLO'

- Smile warmly at the person, making eye contact.

- Look pleased to see the person.

- Say 'Hello' with a warm voice – not in a flat tone that suggests disinterest.

- If I notice something positive that I could mention, I shouldn't ignore it. (Examples are, a stylish new hair cut, a lovely smell of cooking, smart clothes, looking good or really well. However, this does not mean I compliment someone on something I think is awful.)

- Ask the person how he or she is.

- Be prepared to listen to what the person has to say. (It is rude to ask someone how he or she is and then to turn away before the person has had a chance to reply.)

SUGGESTIONS OF RULES FOR SAYING 'GOODBYE'

- Mention what a good time I had, how nice the meal was (if I ate there) and how much I enjoyed spending time with the person.

- Say 'Thank you' to the person for any courtesies shown me. (Such as parents picking me up or taking me home; a friend helping me with my homework; for being such a good friend or a good listener; for serving my favourite food especially for me…)

- Make eye contact with everyone present as I say 'Goodbye', so that no one feels forgotten or left out.

- Smile and raise my hand (or wave) as I leave.

Task: Rules for Specific Social Situations

Under each heading, ask the child to think of the rules that she should follow in the following situations and write these down in her file. If she cannot think of ideas, there are suggestions to help you discuss the situations with the child.

Only a few situations have been given: in life there are a vast number of them and we frequently come across new ones, so it is not possible to prepare for every social event. However, the more practice the child has in dealing with social situations, the more likely she is to develop her own sense of appropriate behaviour. Even as adults we don't always manage to handle new situations gracefully, but the more we think about what we should do and what we should have done, the more likely it is that we will be able to move forward with our social skills.

How should you behave when your friend's relative has died?

- Don't crack jokes.
- Show concern.

- Be sympathetic.
- Depending on how old I am, offer to help.
- Remember she may suffer for a long time after – not just a week or two.
- Offer to talk about it.
- Give physical comfort (such as giving a hug).

How should you behave when someone has won a big competition?

- Show that I am pleased for the person.
- Congratulate the person.
- Ask about the competition in detail to show I am interested in the person's achievement.
- Encourage the person to tell his friends and teacher.

How should you behave when you answer the telephone?

- Be polite.
- Speak very clearly.
- Be serious.
- Offer to take a message, if appropriate.
- Find out whom the person would like to speak to and, if that's not possible, explain why not or tell the person when to ring back.

How should you behave when a friend has lost something important?

- Be sympathetic.
- Ask what it looks like.
- Ask about when he last had the item.
- Offer to help look for it.
- Suggest he tell the teacher or his parents, to ask for further help.

How should you behave when you are out with your parents?

- Be sensible.

- Don't embarrass them.

- Don't do something that will make them feel they have to tell me off in public.

- Live up to their (reasonable) expectations. (This may vary from one family to another.)

How should you behave when you are out with your friends?

- Be happy to join in. (No one likes a grump tagging along.)

- Be fun when appropriate and I feel like it.

- Act in a way that keeps me safe.

- Behave in a way that I approve of – I have to take responsibility for my own behaviour and must not blindly follow what others tell me to do.

How should you behave when your friend is hurt?

- Be sympathetic.

- Check how badly hurt he is and whether I need further help (such as an adult to take him to the doctor's or to hospital).

- Reassure the person.

- Ask the person how he is feeling and whether he is getting any better.

Task: Role-Plays

In the following situations, the child must think of as many ways as she can to make her behaviour positive and to be a good friend, where appropriate. You must be the other person in the situation and help the child to act her part. See if the child can work out what to do without discussing it first. If she has difficulty, repeat the role-play after discussing it with her. Praise all her good ideas and clear loud speech – mumbling isn't nearly as socially effective.

You see a blind man waiting to cross a road (assume you are old enough to do this)

Offer your help – don't assume that he'll want it just because he is blind. You could say, 'Would you like me to take you across the road?' If he agrees, take his arm and lead him across. To check he knows where he is going you could ask, 'Which way do you need to go?' or 'Do you know which way you need to go?' Remember to speak clearly and loudly as he cannot see your lip movements to help him guess your words. If he doesn't answer you it may be that he hasn't heard. You could repeat the questions more loudly.

In the supermarket, the person in front of you has just dropped her shopping – oranges roll all over the floor

Don't wait to ask. Immediately pick up and hand the oranges back to the person or return them to the bag or basket. Make eye contact with the person and receive any thanks with a wide open smile and say, 'That's all right.'

Your friend is crying (because her hamster has died)

Ask your friend what the matter is. Show concern. If she's very upset put your arm around her. Ask her how it happened or when it happened and how old the hamster was. Ask her about the body and burial. Perhaps she'd like you to be there? If you've experienced something similar tell her that you felt awful too and that you understand how she feels.

You bought a pair of shoes but they don't fit properly; you need to take them back to the shop and get your money back (you think that even a different size wouldn't suit as the style is wrong for your foot)

Explain why you have come ('I've come to return these shoes…'), what was wrong with the shoes ('as they don't fit properly') and say that the shoes have not been worn outside ('I haven't worn them outside'). Be firm and polite. If offered another size, refuse. You could say, 'I tried the next size up when I bought these and that was definitely too big. The style doesn't suit me. I want my money back, please.'

Your friend came top in a hard maths test

Congratulate her. ('Well done! That's brilliant – it was so hard! You're very good at maths.') Don't compare her with yourself as that belittles her achievement. Be glad for her coming top.

You are in class when you notice that your teacher has made a spelling mistake on the blackboard (the word should end in 'eous' instead of just 'ous'); you have to tell him

Don't laugh or make the teacher look silly. Put up your hand and wait to be noticed. Then say, 'I think that should be "eous" instead of "ous" at the end.' Wait for your teacher to look at the word and work it out. He ought to thank you for pointing it out to him and if he does, don't smirk. He will not like it if he thinks you are making fun of him in front of the class.

Task: Telephones

Teach the child how to answer the telephone. (She may already have been told what her parents expect of her.) Should she read out the number on answering or should she just say 'Hello'? If she says 'Hello, who is it, who would you like to speak to?' in one long jumble, the person may have difficulty in deciding which question to answer first. A possible method of answering is as follows:

> The telephone rings.
>
> *Child: 'Hello?' (Now wait for the person to speak.)*
>
> The person will now know he's through and will then say whom he wants to speak to.
>
> *Child: 'Who is calling?'*
>
> He should now give his name.
>
> *Child: 'I'm sorry, she's not here at the moment. Can I take a message? (Or: 'Would you like to speak to my dad?')*
>
> He should now give the message (or ask for your dad).
>
> *Child: You should repeat the message to check that you've got it right (or go and get your dad).*

Receiving calls

You need to remember how to answer the telephone, but this is not all. There will be many different situations that crop up where you can't follow the same pattern exactly or it would be inappropriate for you to do so. Do the following exercises and see how good you are at adapting to different situations. Think hard about each exercise so that you understand why you make certain choices.

EXERCISE 1

The telephone rings. You have to answer it as your dad is on the toilet. No one else is at home. The person tells you she wants to speak to your dad.

You don't recognise her voice or her name, when she gives it to you. What do you say?

(a) 'Dad's on the toilet and he usually takes ages.'

(b) 'Can I take your number and get Dad to ring you back in ten minutes?'

(c) 'Could you wait while I get him?'

The worst choice is option (a) as it gives personal information away to someone you don't know. It would be all right if it is said to your grandmother but not all right if the person ringing is your dad's boss – it would embarrass your dad. (He won't want his boss to know that he spends a long time on the toilet.)

Option (b) is fine, if you are able to write down a 'phone number accurately, because it gives your dad time to collect his thoughts as well as not rushing him out of the toilet. If you ask the person's name, your dad has time to think about what the call is about. However, your dad might prefer to make the decision himself about whether or not to rush through his bodily functions.

Option (c) is probably the best, as long as you get the person's name. It gives your dad the choice of whether to speak to the person now or later. Your dad may ask you to ask the person to ring back or to tell her that he won't be long.

EXERCISE 2

Your friend's mum has rung to say she thinks her daughter left her schoolbag at your house. She wants to speak to your mum so that she can arrange to pick it up if it is there. But your mum is out and you have a babysitter who knows nothing about it. What do you say?

(a) 'Mum's out and I've got a babysitter. Would you like me to go and have a look for the bag? If it's here I could ask Mum to give you a ring.'

(b) 'Oh. Mum's not here. I'll get the babysitter.'

(c) 'Mum's not here.'

Option (c) is the least helpful. Option (b) is possible, but then your friend's mum would have to explain all over again and she may not want to speak to the babysitter – you are more likely to know what the bag looks like. It might be simpler to find out whether the bag is there – if it isn't, there's no need to get the babysitter involved. Option (a) is the most helpful. It shows you are thinking for yourself and can take messages. You are also asking the caller if she is happy about you doing that, rather than telling her what you'll do and putting the 'phone down.

EXERCISE 3

Your older brother has asked you to say that he's out if the 'phone is for him because there's someone he's trying to avoid. The 'phone rings and he tells you to answer it. The person at the other end of the 'phone asks to speak to your brother but you can't tell which of his friends it is, so you play safe and say he's out. Now you ask who is it and can you take a message? Too late you realise that it's not the person your brother wanted to avoid and that your brother would want to speak to him. What do you say?

(a) 'I'm sorry, I made a mistake, he is here after all.'

(b) 'He asked me to lie and say he wasn't in because there was someone else he hadn't wanted to speak to.'

(c) 'Oh, hang on, he's just come in.'

Option (b) is not appropriate: your brother may not want anyone to know what he asked you to do – it would also mean he had much explaining to do to his friend. Also, his friend may not be impressed that your brother plays avoidance games. He may suspect your brother of doing it to him some other time. Options (a) and (c) are both possible. However, option (a) is less likely to be accepted as being true. Your brother's friend might ask why you didn't know your own brother was around or why you didn't bother to check properly. The most skilful answer is option (c). Although this is lying, it may be more painful to the people involved if you tell the truth. (If you feel strongly about not lying for your brother, you should refuse to be involved from the beginning.)

Making calls

When you make a 'phone call you need to remember:

- to think about what you want to say
- to dial the number slowly and carefully
- to speak fairly loudly and clearly
- to try to explain what it is that you want, starting at the beginning, not the middle or end of a full explanation.

Task: Tact

Being tactful is quite an advanced social skill. It is being able to read the situation in its entirety and see beyond the obvious. It is then being able to deal with the situation in the most appropriate way so as not to hurt anyone's feelings or make them feel uncomfortable. Tact is hard to master, even for adults, but it is a worthwhile skill that will help the child keep friends and earn her respect from others.

Read the following exercises with the child and discuss what it would be best to do in the circumstance and why. Also, consider what things should *not* be done.

Exercise 1

Grandma gives you some money from her purse just before she leaves and tells you to treat yourself to something.

(a) What should you do?

(b) What should you *not* do?

(a) Thank her and perhaps kiss her. Put the money away.

(b) Count out the money in front of her. Comment on how much she has given you.

You can count the money when Grandma has gone. Examining what she gave you in front of her may embarrass her, especially if she didn't give you very much. It may belittle the gift. Be grateful for any amount that you receive and concentrate on saying goodbye to your Grandma instead of how much money she gave you – or she'll think you care more about money than her.

Exercise 2

You and your friend's family are eating a meal cooked by your friend's dad. You find a hair in your food.

(a) What should you do?

(b) What should you *not* do?

(a) Carefully remove the hair without attracting attention. Put it on the side of your plate.

(b) Say, 'Yuk. There's a hair in my food. I can't eat that, it's disgusting.' Tell everyone to have a good look.

The cook did not deliberately put a hair in your food and he will be embarrassed if he knows his food preparation was not of the most hygienic. (Or he may think it doesn't matter and that it's rude and ungrateful of you to mention it.) It is best quietly and unobtrusively (without being seen or bringing attention to it) to take the hair out of your food and park it at the edge of your plate.

Exercise 3

You are out at a restaurant with your family and your parents' friends celebrating your mum's birthday. You start to ask your mum about that friend of hers she'd told you about who'd had that embarrassing accident, when you suddenly get kicked on your leg. (You weren't supposed to know about it and that particular friend is present.)

(a) What should you do?

(b) What should you *not* do?

(a) Shut up. Concentrate on your food.

(b) Say, 'Ow. That hurt. Why did you kick me?'

If you forget yourself and need to be reminded to be tactful, accept the hint of being elbowed or kicked to stop you mid-sentence. Don't make a fuss about being hurt as you'll make the situation worse and you'll embarrass several people, not just yourself. (In the case of the example, you'd embarrass your mum who had kicked you and everyone knowing she had; your mum for giving away details of her friend's life without permission; the friend herself and everyone who had to see the discomfort it caused.)

In the following situations, see if you can spot the tactless thing the person has said or done and explain why it is tactless.

Situation 1

Dave gets his first pair of glasses and he's thrilled with all the things he can see. The leaves on the trees are no longer just a blur and the flowers have such bright colours. He turns to look at Grandpa and says, 'I never knew you had so many lines.'

(People do not like to be reminded that they are getting old and are developing lines. It makes them feel old and unattractive to have it pointed out to them.)

Situation 2

Sumita looks at a photograph of her brother's friend and compares it with him now as she looks at him and says, 'You had less spots in this photo.'

(People are embarrassed about having spots and do not like to be reminded that they have these blemishes, especially by someone with perfect skin.)

Situation 3

You and your friends are in the kitchen when your mum walks in and helps herself to something in the cupboard. You recognise what she's taking and ask, 'Is that for your constipation?'

(It is not tactful to mention anyone's personal habits or medical problems in front of others. You had the privilege of knowing that your mum suffers from constipation and she may not mind you knowing – but she will mind you telling other people.)

Situation 4 (For boys, use wet dream instead of period)

Your friend told you in confidence that she's just started her first period. She feels very embarrassed and awkward about it and asks you to keep it a secret. Later, when you are queuing for the bus with her and your other friends, you say, 'Has anyone else started their period yet?'

(If you are told something in confidence it means it's a secret. It was up to your friend if she wanted to bring up the subject with her other friends, not you: you betrayed her trust and embarrassed her. Her other friends will ask, 'Who has started her period then?')

Task: Tact in Bypassing the Awful

There will be many occasions in a child's life when she is expected to give an opinion on something, yet won't know how to respond because she thinks the thing is so awful. Discuss the following situations with the child and ask what she could say in the described circumstances. Here, true honesty cannot be given, but neither should she be rude or hurtful: she needs to be sensitive to the other's feelings and tactfully deal with the situation in each case.

1. Your friend has just had his hair dyed red. You think it looks silly on him – even gross. What would you say when you see him?

   Response: 'Oh, you've dyed your hair. It's very bright (or striking). Are you pleased with it?'

2. You are given a meal at a friend's house that you think is disgusting. You cannot eat it. What would you say?

    Response: 'I'm terribly sorry, I'm not used to spicy/Japanese/British food.'

    Or: 'You've gone to so much trouble. I'm terribly sorry but I'm not hungry.'

3. Your friend's just shown you a new dress she's bought. When she tries it on, you see she looks awful in it. What would you say?

    Response: 'I like the dress but it doesn't suit you nearly as much as your old blue one. What do you think?'

Conclusion

Social situations are very fluid – there are no hard and fast rules to fit every occasion and how each one progresses can never be totally predicted. However, it is possible through practice to increase the child's ability to perform well and react to changing circumstances.

Remind the child to be aware of others and to be ready to pick up hints of what is expected of her. Also, she should note how others behave and what it is that makes them a social success or failure. But she should not copy in totality someone else's social style. She needs to absorb all that goes on around her and use all the positive ideas she has in her own special way.

Discuss with the child things that go well and things that go wrong in her social interactions. Tell her what you think is good about the things she has done or said. When things do not go so well ask the child what went wrong and what she should have said or done to make it go well. The sooner after the event that the situation is analysed, the more meaningful it will be to the child. This is particularly important when a child's actions have had some large negative impact on someone else. You could then discuss with the child how she could rescue the relationship or situation.

Chapter 12

Social Safety

This chapter is about social situations where a child may need to protect herself in some way. The exercises given are to help the child think about how to handle those times when she should move away from being polite and helpful: she needs to know that in some circumstances she doesn't have to be polite and can even be rude. (This idea was introduced in Chapter 7, 'Task: When *Can* a Child be Rude?')

Read through the chapter before doing the tasks with the child to assess whether they are appropriate. For example, if the child is never allowed out in public on her own you may decide to skip the task on the 'flasher'. There is no point worrying a child about situations that she is unlikely to meet because of her youth. Likewise, omit something that may upset her sensitive and anxious nature (but don't over-protect).

Over-protection can bring problems. If you have not given a child any idea of dangers or how to protect herself, then she is ill equipped to look after herself and may be completely fazed when something worrying does happen. The problem is, very often when we assume that children are completely safe there may be an unknown factor that presents itself and then a child's inadequate safety training may cause disaster.

You need to find the correct balance for the child that is appropriate to her home environment. This means considering where she lives, whether she goes to school unaccompanied, whether she lives in the country or a town, which areas she needs to walk or travel through, whether she goes out with a group of friends or alone. What you cover should also relate to her age. For example, a seven-year-old is not likely to be going to a night club with her friends – but she might answer the 'phone.

A 16-year-old could work through all the tasks in this chapter. To make it a little harder for the older child, ask her to answer the tasks without consulting the multiple-choice suggestions. Then, when she has provided a solution of her own, discuss its merits and compare it with the given suggestions.

Parental Pages on Social Safety

Photocopiable for professional use within the institution that bought the book, to use to help parents keep their child safe.

Task: Parents: Personal Safety Rules

This task is for parents to do with the help of the professional.

Discuss with your child what rules she has already been given to do with keeping her safe. Add to these any that you think are missing. Then write a list in your child's folder.

Suggested rules for children

- Never go anywhere without permission.
- Know my own telephone number.
- Know my own address.
- Know, or carry on me, my parents' work telephone numbers.
- Always tell my parents where I am going.
- Always tell my parents whom I am with.
- Understand whether I am to walk home alone or wait to be picked up.
- Understand what time I am to be home.
- If anything happens to change something, I must let my parents know. (For example, if I am at one friend's house and we decide to go on to another friend's house, I should ring or pop home first to let my parents know where I am. Or if I'm supposed to be walked home by my friend's older sister but she refuses, I should ring to let my parents know and so they can tell me what to do.)

- Wear a watch if I have to get myself home by a certain time.
- If someone has done something to upset me or make me feel uneasy about being with her, I must tell my parents. (This includes being bullied or if someone has touched me in a way that makes me feel uncomfortable.)
- Don't talk to strangers or give them any information about where I live or what my name is. (Although my parents often chat to complete strangers in a dentist's waiting room or on a train platform, I know they are old enough and experienced enough to work out what is safe and what isn't. I am not.)
- If I have something important to tell my parents and they are too busy to listen, I must make them listen. I must explain it's important and not let myself be put off.

A child also has a right to expect parents to follow some safety rules. Discuss what they may be with your child and write them in her folder too.

Suggested rules for parents

- Be consistent with your expectations.
- Expect your child's rules to be followed.
- Be prepared to listen to your child.
- Try to give time to talk to your child each day to find out how things went and to give your child an opportunity to tell you if anything has upset her.
- When your child goes out for the first time with someone (a relative, close friend or someone new), ask her how it went and look for any reaction that worries you. Then gently pursue it.
- Do not get angry with your child for telling you about something that has gone wrong – instead use the situation positively to work out why it went wrong, how it could

have been made right and discuss what to do in the future. Show how pleased you are that your child is safe. If you get angry with her she might not tell you the next time something happens and you won't be aware of possible danger.

- Have contingency plans. (For example, if you are not there when your child gets home from school, what should she do?)

Task: Parents: Contingency Plans

This task is for parents to do with the help of the professional.

Discuss with your child various situations she might come across and ask her what she would do if things did not go according to what she'd expected. It is important not to tell your child straight away what you think she should do, because she needs to develop the skill to think things through herself. Practising verbally with a caring adult, in a safe environment, gives your child the confidence to act later on her own and you the confidence to know that she can work things out sensibly.

Example 1

You get home from school one day to find no one at home. This has never happened before, so you haven't been told what to do, and you do not have a key. What would you do?

SUGGESTIONS

Think about:

- where my mum or dad might be
- whether they mentioned going anywhere last night or this morning
- whether they had arranged to meet me somewhere after school (for example, to buy me new shoes)
- their habits (does my mum or dad often spend time with a neighbour? Might he or she have forgotten the time? Could I try knocking on the neighbour's door to find out?)
- whether it's the time Mum or Dad get home from work. Might their bus or train have been delayed or cancelled?

Choose an action:

- If I can contact them by mobile 'phone and I have one too I should try that (or go to a call box to ring their mobile number if I don't have one myself).

- If I have their work numbers and there is a call box nearby (or a friend's or neighbour's 'phone) I should try that.

Otherwise:

- If I think they may be home soon, I should wait patiently in the garden, if I have one, or out of sight from the street, around the side of the house.

- I could go to a trusted neighbour's house or a nearby friend's house – but I should leave a note to tell my parents where I am. I could ask a neighbour or friend for pen and paper and take the note back – or try 'phoning to leave a message if they have an answering machine or voice mail service.

- I could try 'phoning at frequent intervals to catch them as soon as they come home to tell them where I am if I have gone to someone else's house.

- If there is a police station near my home, I could go in and wait there.

NOTE

When walking to your friend's house, walk confidently. Don't look scared or unsure of yourself – this would immediately tell a bad person that something isn't right and that you are not on familiar territory. People who look confident are much more likely to be left alone.

Don't go into the home of anyone you don't feel comfortable with, even if it's pouring with rain.

(Much of the child's safety in the above situation depends on her being able to use a 'phone. She should be taught, as soon as possible, how to use a pay 'phone as well as using private and mobile 'phones – if the family has them. Although the next situation is also 'phone dependent, a child who is old enough to go out alone in a town should already know how to use public telephones.)

Example 2

You arrange to go to the cinema with a friend. You are supposed to meet him outside the cinema complex at 1 pm but he isn't there. By 1.30 pm, you are very worried that he's not coming and you feel uncomfortable about the curious glances people are giving you. What should you do?

SUGGESTIONS

- Ask myself if I'm definitely waiting in the right place.
- Look around to see if he's waiting somewhere else by mistake.
- Telephone his home to ask if he's left and at what time.
- If there's no answer, ring home to ask what I should do.
- If there's no one home, I should go back and wait for another 20–30 minutes.
- If he still hasn't come, I should try ringing his home again, then mine.
- If I have no contact with anyone, I should assume he's not coming and go home.
- If he should turn up and I've left a message on anyone's 'phone to say I'm alone at the cinema, I should ring back to tell the person I'm safe and that he has arrived.

Task: Parents: Telephone Safety

This task is for parents to do with the help of the professional.

Most people have a telephone in the home. Your child needs to know that she should not give out information to someone she is not absolutely sure should have it. If in any doubt, she should always consult you or another adult.

Exercise 1

You answer the 'phone and when you ask who the person wants to speak to he says 'Sharon'. But there is no one of that name in your house. What do you say?

(a) 'I think you've got the wrong number.'

(b) 'There's no Sharon, only...' (Give your name and then your parents' names.)

(c) 'I'll get Mum.'

Options (a) and (c) are both good. With option (a), you are dealing with the wrong number yourself, which would be the most convenient choice if your mum or dad were busy. However, if you are in any doubt over a caller and you are young, it is probably better to get an adult on the line, especially if the caller starts to ask questions. Option (b) is the worst. It is dangerous to start chatting to an unknown caller or to give out information about you or your family. Once it's clear he has no connection with your household, cut the conversation short and hang up.

Exercise 2

Someone rings. You don't recognise the voice. Instead of telling you whom he wants to speak to he asks for your address and then wants to know how old you are. What do you say?

(a) 'Who is calling?' (If he's dishonest he probably won't say. If he does, you can then pass the 'phone over to an adult.) 'I'll get my dad for you.'

(b) '29 East Mill Crescent. I'm eight.'

(c) You don't get into conversation. You just put the 'phone down.

Options (a) and (c) are both acceptable. If you have an adult in the house then it is probably best to hand over a suspicious 'phone call to him or her. If you are alone, because you are older, just put the 'phone down (or if you are effectively alone because the only adult present is in the bath).

Option (b) is dangerous. Never give out personal details to a stranger. If he were a friend he would know where you lived. An adult should never ask a child such details in any case. So, if he is a genuine caller, he would expect to be handed over to an adult.

Task: Parents: Computer Safety

This task is for parents to do with the help of the professional.

Computers are becoming part of our everyday lives. Even if your child does not have an Internet-compatible computer at home, she can have access to one through school, someone else's computer, the local library or an Internet-café. Your child needs to be aware that she should not give any information that identifies where she lives or goes to school, or her telephone number, to another unknown person. She may also wish to withhold her surname, especially if it is very unusual and easily traceable through directory enquiries.

NOTE

Your child should always ask your permission before agreeing to meet a stranger she has met on the Internet. You might feel more at ease if you went with your child to meet her new contact. Although the person may have seemed friendly and safe while chatting in the Internet you child needs to understand that this does not necessarily follow. She must be very wary about meeting the person. it would be a good idea if she got the person's full name, telephone number and address and speaks to him over the 'phone before agreeing to meet (to check the number is correct). She should give you all the person's details before she goes out.

The following exercise has not been included because it is OK to meet strangers, but to raise awareness of the possible dangers to those who have already done so or are thinking of doing so.

Exercise 1

You are 16, have met someone on the Internet and have been sending one another emails for some time. He requests a meeting. Where would you arrange to meet?

(a) At your house.

(b) At his house.

(c) In a local park.

(d) In a large shopping centre that you know well.

Option (a) is not a safe choice. You have no idea what the person is really like through writing alone. You should only let him know where you live once you feel comfortable about being with him. Even if it turns out to be all right on the first occasion, he may unexpectedly call on you when you are home alone. You should never invite someone home when you are alone until you know him or her well.

Option (b) is not safe either. You might not know the area in which he lives, so might not be able to get away in a hurry. You also do not know his family or whether anyone else will be at home. You might be trapped inside his house.

Option (c) might be OK if the park is crowded but often there are lonely places, so option (d) is the best. In a familiar crowded shopping centre, you are always surrounded by others and in calling distance of help and know how to get away. It is also an anonymous place: you need not need risk your home address being known and you can choose a place that is accessible to both of you but far enough away from your home territory so that he can't bump into you by chance and follow you home.

Exercise 2

You receive an email that looks like it was sent to you by mistake. What do you do?

(a) Delete it and forget about it.

(b) Reply to the author to tell the person not to send you emails any more.

(c) Send the email to your Internet provider and complain that someone has got your email address from somewhere.

Option (a) is the best option and the easiest. If you choose option (b) and reply to the author, you are sending the author your email address with your name on. This may have been what the person hoped. Some mistaken emails are computer-generated and sent out in the hundreds. Only if you reply to a mistaken email are you identifying yourself to the mystery person who has then been given the means of pestering you further. (Your email address is automatically attached to your outgoing emails.) Option (c) is probably only necessary if you have a repeated problem – but you could contact your Internet provider if you wish.

Note that there is also the danger of importing a computer virus if an email from an unknown source, programmed to damage, is opened. This could seriously affect your computer.

Task: Parents: Out and About

This task is for parents to do with the help of the professional.

A child needs to learn to be streetwise and aware of what's going on: but without being scared. Parental control needs to be gradually let go, giving the child more freedom as she gets older and discussing what she would do if certain things happened. This should give her the confidence to grow to be independent at the same rate as parents are willing to let go.

The exercises here are given in ascending order of age, the ones more suited to the very young first, followed by those more suited to older children.

Exercise 1

You are in a very large supermarket and are distracted by a toy on a shelf and do not notice that your dad moves on ahead. He has not realised you are no longer with him. When you look up, you find you are all alone. What would you do?

(a) Stay where you are.

(b) Go to the customer service desk and tell them you are lost.

(c) Leave the shop and wait for your dad by the car.

(d) Walk around the shop looking for him.

(e) Ask another shopper to help you.

(f) Ask a uniformed shop assistant to help you.

Option (c) is the worst choice. You should never leave the shop. There are more dangers in a car park than in the shop. You could get run over; it might be lonely and no one would notice if someone tried to take you away; you might be waiting for ages because your dad would look for you inside the shop.

Option (d) is likely to make you panic – and your father. It might be ages before you find one another. It also gives the opportunity for some nasty person to see you looking lost and frightened to say he's seen your dad outside and that he will take you to him – to get you away from your dad and into more danger.

You could choose option (a) and stay where you are. Your dad should know to go back to the place where he saw you last. However, if anything happens to worry you, shout out 'Dad!' or go to a shop assistant.

If you choose option (e), don't let the person take hold of you – you can scream if this happens – and check that the person is taking you straight to a shop assistant. Members of the public should not try to help you themselves, they should pass you onto someone in authority – such as the police, but in this case an employee of the supermarket. However, option (e) is not recommended.

Options (b) and (f) are the best choices. If you choose option (f), the assistant should take you straight to customer services in any case. From there, they will be able to contact your dad over the public address system.

Exercise 2

You are in a toy shop. Your dad wants to look in a different section of the shop and leaves you in the board games section. He tells you to stay there and he will come to you in a few minutes. While he is away, an adult or older child (who is another customer, not a shop assistant) comes up to you and starts asking you questions and then suggests you leave the shop with her to buy some sweets. What would you do?

(a) Say, 'No thank you.'

(b) Shout to a shop assistant that you don't know this person and she's bothering you.

(c) Tell her to leave you alone.

(d) Get away from her and walk around the shop hoping to find your dad.

Option (b) is the best choice. It is also better to get a witness to see the person. Behaviour like this ought to be reported to the police.

No one should suggest you leave the shop together. Options (a) and (c) might not be enough to get rid of her – and even if she leaves you alone for now, she might try it on with someone else. It is best to get the police involved.

Option (d) is not a safe choice. You might not be able to find your dad right away (unless you can see him and you shout to him as you go), and the person might follow you. It is best to stay in the area he expects you to be in. Also, if you have to pass the exit while moving out of your section into another, it may give the person the opportunity of pulling you out quickly. Stay away from any exit doors. You are safest in the shop.

If in any doubt, scream and shout and make much noise to keep yourself safe! If the person grabs hold of you, scream, kick and scratch. No one has a right to do that. Do not be afraid of people looking over to you to see what the noise is about – that's exactly what you need to get their help.

Exercise 3

You are in a crowded changing room at a public swimming pool and your dad has gone to the toilets while leaving you to get changed. You have just finished changing and feel uncomfortable about being on your own with so many people about and Dad's been gone a while. You're not sure if he's still there. You go to the toilet area but there are loads of cubicles and many children and dads around. You feel frightened and desperate for Dad. What would you do?

   (a) Say, 'Dad?'

   (b) Shout, 'Dad!'

   (c) Shout, 'Dad, it's David Bloggs!'

   (d) Shout, 'Eddie Bloggs, where are you?'

With option (a), you probably won't be heard and, even if you were, with so many other children with dads, how would your dad know it was you? A single word is not much to go on with so much background noise – he may not recognise your voice. He might think it's some other child asking for his dad.

✓

Option (b) is better, but there is still room for doubt – you may get someone else's dad answering you and that's not what you want. Your dad might think you're still in the changing area.

Options (c) and (d) are equally good. Your dad will know straight away that it's you and will be able to give you a reassuring shout back.

What you mustn't do is leave the changing rooms – either to go into the pool or into the rest of the building. You must stay in the area where your dad expects to find you. Your dad would not have left the changing room without telling you.

Exercise 4

You are in the park with a friend. A group of older children approach and ask if the two of you want to join them at the other end of the park. You don't know them (or not very well) and have never played with them before. What would you do?

(a) Refuse to go.

(b) Say you can't because you're just leaving. Your parents are expecting you back. (You then turn to go.)

(c) Say 'OK' and go with them.

(d) Find out more about why they want you to go to the other end of the park.

Option (b) is the safest. Mentioning adults who might come and look for you if you are late might get them to give up. By leaving the park you are making it clear that you are not going to be persuaded to change your mind. When you get home you should discuss the situation with your parents to hear what they think about it.

Option (a) might mean they try to persuade you to change your mind and you might feel forced to go with them if you can't think up a reasonable excuse. Option (c) is dangerous. You should not agree to go anywhere with people you don't know and people your parents do not know. Option (d) is not very safe either. You have shown you are interested and with persistence they will know they can probably force you to go.

Just because the strangers are children themselves it does not mean they are safe. Safe people are usually people you know and trust. Many children bully and it would be unusual for children older than you suddenly to want to play nice games with you, a younger child: usually they wouldn't be seen dead in the company of youngsters.

If your friend wants to go but you are not happy about her or your safety, *don't go with her.* You cannot help her, if she does need help, by going too. Go straight home and tell an adult what has happened and then the adult can go and look for your friend. Do not put yourself at risk. Walking away from her might make her think twice about going alone with them and so she might follow you back. In any case, tell an adult about what happened.

Exercise 5

You are on a crowded beach with your mum. She has fallen asleep and you are bored. You see an ice cream van not far away and want to buy one with the pocket money you have with you. You have never done this alone before (in other words, you are still quite young and are not a strapping teenager). What would you do?

(a) Wait until your mum wakes up and hope that the van stays that long.

(b) Go by yourself to buy the ice cream.

(c) Wake your mum up to ask permission to go alone to buy the ice cream.

Option (b) is dangerous. A child alone is easily spotted and someone might try to take advantage of that and whisk you away. You might also not be in calling distance of your mum if things should go wrong. You might think that, as the beach is crowded, it would be safe, but this may not be so and if your mum woke up to find you gone she'd be frantic with worry.

Choose either option (a) or (c) depending on whether your mum needs her sleep.

Exercise 6

You are out shopping on your own in your home town. You see a group of teenagers around another teenager and it looks as though they are threatening him. What would you do?

(a) Shout at them from a safe distance to leave the boy alone.

(b) Go up to the group and tell them off for bullying.

(c) Ignore what you've seen and walk the other way.

(d) Go into a nearby shop and tell them what you have seen. Ask them to help the boy. (If necessary, they could call the police.)

Option (a) is not very likely to achieve anything although it might attract the attention of responsible adult shoppers and get them to intervene. Option (b) is dangerous – they might start to pick on you as well or leave the boy altogether and concentrate on you. You would be near enough to be grabbed by them and hurt. Keep well away.

Option (c) is not very humane and may bother you for some time to come – you would wonder what had happened to the boy and whether you could have helped in some way. Option (d) is the safest and the best way to help the boy. Adults can deal better with a gang of bullies than another child – and the bullies need never know who it was that got them involved.

Exercise 7

You are out on your own and see a man mistreating his dog. He has just given it a hard kick and it yelped with pain. What would you do?

(a) Take a good look at the man and the dog and go to the police station to tell the police about it. You'd be able to give a good description of them as you looked carefully at both of them.

(b) Go and tell the man exactly what you think of him.

(c) Ignore it and pretend you didn't see or hear anything.

(d) Go home and tell your dad and ask him to ring the police or RSPCA (Royal Society for the Prevention of Cruelty to Animals).

Option (b) is the most dangerous thing to do. If the man is not bothered about hurting his dog, he may not be too worried about hurting you either. Option (c) does not help the poor dog – and you might feel guilty about not doing anything for some time to come.

Options (a) and (d) are both possible solutions to the problem. In either case, it helps to get a good description of both man and dog. It may be that you are too young to go to the police on your own, in which case you could go home first and then ask an adult to take you to, or to 'phone, the local police station. Since dog owners need to have a licence, the police might be able to trace the owner from their records.

Exercise 8

You are out on your own and need to catch a train to get home. There is a drunk man on your platform, staggering up and down, clutching a bottle in a brown paper bag. He comes over to where you are sitting. There is one other person waiting at the end of the platform. What would you do?

(a) Tell the man to go away.

(b) Leave the platform and tell the ticket collector or ticket seller that there is a drunk man on the platform and you don't feel safe.

(c) Go and stand next to the other waiting passenger (but don't make conversation with him).

(d) Stay where you are, ignoring the drunk man, hoping he'll go away, making sure you don't make eye contact.

Option (a) is likely to enrage the man and, as he is drunk, he may not be able to behave rationally (sensibly) and his behaviour may be unpredictable. It is definitely not safe to choose this option.

Options (b), (c) and (d) are all possible choices, depending on how old you are and how confident you feel. If you are young and have only just started going out on your own, choose option (b). The next safest is option (c) – but the other passenger might not necessarily be safe either, so don't get friendly with the person. Option (d) is probably safe for an older teenager, used to such situations. However, if you were to be the only one on the platform, you should leave to get help. (It is an offence to be drunk in public – the railway employees could call the police.)

Exercise 9

You are walking home through the park in the daytime. There are a few others ahead of you. A man walks out from behind some bushes, holding something in his hand. He keeps lowering his eyes, expecting you to look down. When you do, you are shocked to see it's his penis. What would you do?

(a) Shout to the people ahead of you: 'Hey, this man's showing me his willy!'

(b) Run away and never tell anyone about it as you're too shocked.

(c) Burst out laughing and say, 'That's a bit small isn't it?' (Men like to think they have big willies.) Or, 'You'd better put it away before it catches cold.' Then walk off without looking behind you.

(d) Ignore the man and his penis and go to the nearest police station to report that you've seen a 'flasher'.

Option (a) is fine for an immediate response. Men 'flash' at young children to shock them and if you don't behave like a shocked and timid child, you have taken his enjoyment away and have not rewarded him for his inappropriate behaviour.

Option (b) is definitely not right. You need to talk to someone about it otherwise it may worry you and it does not stop the man from frightening other children. Option (c) may annoy the man – although it might be fine for an adult to say these things, it is risky for a child.

Option (d) is essential. The police need to know about people who expose their private parts and they may even be able to pick up the man that same afternoon to charge him and prevent him from doing it to others. Options (d) and (a) together is the best choice.

When reporting to the police, you will need to remember what the man looked like and what he was wearing. If you can't remember, you will still need to go to report the crime. If you don't want to go to the police station alone, get an adult to go with you. However, the sooner you report the crime the more likely it is that the police will spot the man the same day, accosting other children.

Exercise 10

You are at a night club or disco with friends. You have a row with the person you are meant to be going home with and she leaves you there to make your own way home. You have never been allowed to go home late at night on your own before and you know you will get into trouble from your parents for being alone. You think they will blame you. Also, you have hardly any money. What do you do?

(a) Order a taxi and tell the driver that your parents will pay the fare when you get home.

(b) Decide to risk going home by yourself, on foot or using public transport.

(c) Ring your parents up from the club and ask them to come and get you (assuming it is close enough to walk to or they have transport).

(d) Ask people leaving the club if they are going your way home.

Option (b) is not something you should consider, even if you are worried about getting into trouble. Your personal safety is more important than a telling off. You could possibly ring the parents of the friend who let you down and ask for their help, but your parents would probably still hear about it and what happened is not something you should hide – they need to know if there's a chance it might happen again.

Option (d) is not at all safe. You must not entrust yourself to complete strangers. There is the additional worry that, if they have a car to give you a lift in and have been drinking, they may crash.

The safest by far is option (c). If your parents want you to get a taxi home they will tell you – but most likely they would like to come and get you themselves. It is safer for you to wait inside the club until they arrive, rather than on the street.

If you do end up getting a taxi, and you're female, you could ask the company if they could assign a female driver to you. Otherwise, ask for the registration number of the car so that you don't approach every car that comes slowly by – drivers may think you are a soliciting prostitute. Always check that the driver has been told your name (you have to give your name to the company operator when you book the taxi) to avoid getting into the wrong cab.

Conclusion

It is important for a child to know that she has permission to do whatever is necessary to keep herself safe. She can break all the social rules if she is, or thinks she is, in danger. All can be explained later if a mistake is made. It is better that a child listens to her gut instincts and acts on them rather than suppressing all feelings of unease and putting herself at risk.

For further practice, parent and child could be encouraged to play 'What if?' games. For example, if the child has swimming lessons, her parent might ask her, 'What would you do if I wasn't there when you got out?' This gives the child more confidence in working out how to keep herself safe, and the parent feedback on how well his or her child understands the principles of personal safety.

Chapter 13

Communication Skills for Improving the Quality of the Child's Relationships

Communication is about a child getting her meaning across in the best way. This means being easily understood, not trying to use clever words that she might stumble on or that others might not understand.

Body language and its use in reinforcing the words someone uses has already been covered in some detail. This chapter is concerned with getting the whole message across – verbally, with complementary use of body language. It is also about trying to understand the other person's point of view to allow full understanding of the situation.

Verbal communication is a flow of information between two or more people. This may be factual information (for example, when the next train leaves for Paddington), or it may be emotional information (for example, telling someone she is angry with him because he ignored her when she was with her baby brother).

Many problems in relationships arise out of poor communication skills and the unwillingness of one party to communicate (an example of this is sulking rather than discussing the problem openly and trying to sort it out).

Task: Communicating with Different People

A child will communicate with different people in many different ways. The strategies she adopts at home may be different to those she uses with her friends. Ask her to tell you the names of people with whom she regularly communicates and to describe how she communicates and behaves with each. How does her verbal and body language change? Are there any phrases she only uses with one group of people (for example, friends)? Write the details in the child's file, using the headings given below. (Some suggested answers have been given.)

PEOPLE I COMMUNICATE WITH	HOW I BEHAVE
Parents	I don't swear.
	I am very familiar with them: I tease and play jokes on them.
	I am loving towards them: I often touch them and hug them.
	I am often very sweet towards them to get my own way.
	I resent their interference and sometimes act as though I'm better than they are.
	I ignore them most of the time as they don't understand me.
	I take out my anger on them as they frustrate me.
Teachers	I behave formally: I don't call them by their first names and I am polite at all times.
	I don't swear in front of them.
	I am aggressive/timid in their presence.
Sports coach	I don't always do what I'm told – at least, not straight away.
	I often stick my tongue out when she's not looking – or stick my fingers up at her.
	I do everything with bad grace – I don't like sports.
	I try to do my best to impress her so that I will be picked for the team.
Friends	I am rough with them – we tackle each other for fun.

I show off when I'm with them.

I tease and play tricks on them.

I laugh a lot when I'm with them – we have great fun together.

I often swear at them or when I'm with them.

I often say 'Shut up' or 'Get out of my face' and 'It's cool'.

Someone you're attracted to

I try to catch his eye all the time.

I'm clumsy in his presence and keep dropping things.

My words get jumbled up and they come out wrong.

I twiddle with my hair and keep wanting to check that I look OK.

I keep looking round in the hope that I see him.

I have a ready smile on my lips.

I laugh nervously whenever he speaks to me.

Neighbours

I'm polite.

I'm not very friendly – I've got nothing to chat to them about.

I avoid them if I can get out of their way before they see me as it's easier.

Every personality interacts in a different way with other personalities – it's part of what makes us unique. Also, our personality interacts in a different way to the roles other people have. For example, we have learnt that teachers are not fun people to play chase with at break-times and they are not our 'equal' in that they have a position of authority over us.

*What reasons can the child give for why she behaves in different
ways with the different people she's mentioned? (Discuss only)*

SUGGESTIONS

Parents

If they are strict you probably pretend to be well
behaved for an easier life and instead do more things
behind their back.

If you are very aggressive or you have laid-back
parents, you may feel you like walking all over them
and that they can't stop you doing what you like.

You may love your parents and want to show
them this at all times, particularly if you are timid
and insecure and are very dependent on them. Here,
you may be showing anxiety at not being cared for
and needing reassurance.

Teachers

You may be awed by anyone in authority so behave
well, watch your language and are very polite.

Or you may fight against the school system and
be antagonistic to everyone in authority, swearing
and being aggressive in manner to show the teacher
he or she has not got the better of you.

Or you may have a favourite teacher whom you
admire, so you hang on every word that's uttered
and quote the things she says. You might fall over
yourself to help her in any way you can.

Sports coach

You may hate sports so much that you take it out on
the coach.

Or you may feel free from pressure once out of
the classroom and let yourself go and consequently
become more aggressive.

Or this may be the only area where you excel and
so you try your hardest and are at your most
co-operative.

Friends	These are people for you to thoroughly be yourself with. They are far less judgemental than any other group of people you spend time with. So, you may be more outgoing and willing to take more risks with your language and your behaviour. You can be as silly or emotional as you like. You may show many sides to your character over a period of time and friends will be much more tolerant of your changes in mood.
Someone you're attracted to	You probably want to be on your best behaviour and look your best at all times, although you might have a tendency to show off. Your nervousness might make you clumsier unless you are used to having partners, in which case you might openly flirt with someone you are attracted to and behave more confidently in his or her presence.
Neighbours	You may have a very good relationship with your neighbours. They may be parents of your best friend and you may have spent much of your childhood in their house, in which case you are likely to look favourably upon them and enjoy exchanging a few words. Or you may see them as busybodies who are always checking up on you and then telling tales to your parents. Or you may simply not like talking to people you don't know well as you don't know what to say, so prefer to avoid meeting them whenever possible to save yourself embarrassment.

Task: Understanding Needs and Learning to Negotiate

Very often, relationships are not as strong or as fulfilling as they might be because whenever a conflict situation arises, neither side is prepared to compromise. Sometimes it is easy to think of a quick solution to the conflict as in the example and exercises below.

Example

You want to watch television but your parents have asked you to do your homework. You suggest watching the end of your programme before doing your homework but your parents refuse.

> Problem: Your parents want you to do your homework now, to ensure it is finished before your bedtime. You, however, want to watch a particular programme.

> *Compromise:* *You'll start your homework immediately if your parents tape the end of the programme for you. If you finish your work in good time you can see it that night, otherwise you'll have to wait until the next day.*

The following exercises give examples of conflict situations. Discuss the best compromise with the child.

Exercise 1

You have a friend round to play. She wants to play 'Twister' but you want to play 'Ker-Plunk'. What do you do?

> *Compromise:* *As she's the guest, play her choice first and yours second.*

Exercise 2

Your dad is cooking your tea and insists that you have peas as you need to eat vegetables with your meal. You hate peas. What do you do?

> *Compromise:* *You know that you must have some sort of vegetable. Ask for raw carrot instead – it doesn't need cooking so may be easier*

for your dad to prepare. If you're old enough, offer to prepare it yourself. Or ask to eat your peas with tomato sauce or butter to make them taste better.

Exercise 3

You want to go to the cinema on your own with a friend for the first time. Your parents won't let you. What do you do?

> *Compromise: Ranting and raving won't get you anywhere (or it shouldn't!). Neither should you start sneaking out on your own without their permission. Ask them what they are worried about. Point out that they know your friend well. Suggest they take you to the cinema and pick you up afterwards. Understand that it might be hard for your parents to let go at each stage of your independence because they worry about you.*

Task: Understanding the Other's Point of View

Sometimes the situation is more involved and, before any compromise is suggested, it is important for each party to understand the other's point of view and how he or she feels. This means that both parties must communicate with each other. Once each side does understand the other's point of view, negotiation can begin to bring about some sort of compromise – a halfway solution to a problem.

Ask the child to think about her relationships and ask herself where the weaknesses are. Then discuss what she could do about them, using the example below as a framework.

Example

You often have arguments with your parents, with both sides shouting. The arguments usually end with you storming upstairs in tears.

Are the arguments always about the same sort of thing? (For example, what time you have to be in at night or not doing your homework in front of the television.)

SUGGESTION

- Write down what you want and what your parents want.
- Jot down your reasons for having your own way and ask your parents for their reasons for not letting you have it.
- Then sit down calmly and discuss the situation, explaining how you feel.
- Listen to how they feel about it.
- Can you think of a compromise that would satisfy you both?

The aim of the exercise is for you to be very clear about what you want and why, and how you feel. This helps your understanding of yourself and your needs. It is then your responsibility to communicate these needs to your parents or whomever is obstructing you.

Then, it is your duty to *listen* to the other person so that you *understand* his or her point of view. You cannot expect someone to listen to all your needs without giving the person a chance to have his or her say. Ideally, both you and the other person should then discuss the areas on which you agree, and differ, and come to some sort of compromise.

This is using your communication skills to move forward and reach a better level of understanding of yourself and others – and they of you. There is communication breakdown when neither party listens to what the other has to say, or if their needs and feelings are not spoken about.

Task: Don't Expect People to Guess Your Needs

Often, a child might throw a wobbly because something has gone wrong and she blames it on someone else (often parents or siblings). Discuss with the child situations when this has happened, using the examples below as a framework on which to build. Then talk about what the other person should have said to her, and she to him or her, so that she sees a way out of the situation for next time. Write the suggestions in her file, together with the initial problem.

Example 1

You tell your parents that you don't want to go to school anymore. They say, 'Nonsense, of course you must go.'

Your parents' point of view:	You are being lazy or are just trying it on so that you get do something you prefer, such as playing with your new computer game.
Your point of view:	You are scared to go to school because you are being bullied.
Way forward:	You must explain to your parents what's been happening to make you feel like this so that they can deal with it.

Example 2

You are going shopping with a friend. You let him choose which shops you want to visit and when you get home your parents ask if you've found a pair of trainers. You fly into a rage and shout 'No!' and stomp upstairs.

Your parents' point of view:	They were showing interest in your shopping trip and had asked politely if you'd got what you'd wanted. They did nothing to deserve being shouted at.
Your point of view:	You'd gone shopping for trainers and had come home without any because you'd let your friend dictate where you went. You should have told him

what you needed and asked to visit a shoe or sports shop. You are angry and disappointed that it hadn't worked out.

Way forward: Be honest with your parents. Explain that the shopping trip was a failure for you because you hadn't the courage to speak up to visit the right shops. Say you are angry with yourself for not speaking out and with your friend for not asking you where you wanted to go. Explain that you're grumpy, although not with them, and that you need to be alone for a while.

Note to parents

Just as you expect your child to be open and honest with you, so must you be with her. If you have had a bad day and are tired and grumpy, explain to your child how you are feeling and suggest that she leaves you be, because you don't want to take out your bad day on her.

Task: Feedback

Feedback is finding out how you are doing and letting others know how they are doing. For example, if you are pleased with the child, you will reward her behaviour by smiling at her (and cuddling her if you are her parent) – you are giving her positive feedback. She knows that you approve because of the pleased or loving way you behave towards her.

Two of the most important things about communication are giving the right feedback messages and being able to receive them – that is, noticing them and correctly interpreting them. You can then change your behaviour in relation to these messages either to stop what you are doing (when it is negative feedback) or to do more of the same (if it is positive feedback).

Discuss what feedback is with the child and then work through the questions below with her.

Positive feedback

Positive feedback must be rewarding. The person on the receiving end must experience pleasure or pride at receiving such communication messages.

HOW DO YOU SHOW POSITIVE FEEDBACK WHEN:

- *you approve of something someone's done?*

  Say 'I'd have done the same' or 'You've done really well' or 'That's brilliant' or, 'You tried your hardest – no one could ask for more.'

- *you are interested in what the person is saying?*

  Smile and nod my head.
  Say things like, 'Really?' or, 'I never knew that' in an interested way.
  Make much eye contact.

- *the person has done a very big favour for you*

  Kiss the person.
  Hug the person.
  Give the person a gift.
  Enthusiastically thank the person.

Negative feedback

When negative feedback is used, you are letting someone know that he or she is behaving inappropriately. Negative feedback must tell the person that you are displeased with her and that you want her to stop doing whatever it is she's started. It must inform the person that you disapprove of her behaviour or her actions and must try to prevent her from continuing in the same vein. Negative feedback can be blatant ('Shut up!') or subtle (ignoring a comment you don't like).

HOW DO YOU SHOW NEGATIVE FEEDBACK WHEN:

- *you disapprove of something someone's done*

  Ignore it.
  Purse my lips at it. Sneer at it.
  Say 'That wasn't very clever of you' or, 'I'd have expected better of you.'

- *you are not interested in   Look bored.
  what the person's saying*   Look around the room.
                               Avoid the person's eyes.
                               Yawn. Say, 'Really?' in a sarcastic way
                               as though I couldn't have cared less.
                               Make the right noises ('Mm. Really?')
                               but in a flat, uninterested way.

- *the person has done   Be angry.
  something against you*   Say something horrible.
                               Say I don't want to see him or her
                               again.
                               Start rumours in revenge.
                               Make rude signs at the person.
                               Swear at the person.
                               Threaten the person against doing it
                               again. (Although these are all examples
                               of negative feedback, they are
                               aggressive and therefore not examples
                               of positive behaviour.)

As well as behaving in a certain way in response to how another behaves, negative feedback can vary depending on the situation you are in. Try to think of all the occasions when negative feedback has been used in the following situations:

In school: The teacher raising his eyebrows warningly or in
                      (pretend) shocked surprise to control my behaviour.
                      Ignoring a deliberately silly answer.
                      Ignoring my raised hand because I was behaving
                      badly.
                      Slightly shaking his head at me when he catches my
                      eye to stop me from doing something. Informing me
                      he wants to see me at the end of the lesson – it acts
                      as a warning against further bad behaviour and lets
                      me know I've been seen.
                      Shouting.
                      Giving a detention (secondary school).
                      Giving lines or copying from a book as punishment.

At home: Telling me I've lost my pocket money because of my behaviour.

Having privileges taken away (for example, not being allowed to watch television or to go and play with someone).

Shouting at me.

Ignoring me.

Being sent to my room.

Being grounded (not allowed to go out for a certain length of time).

Socially: My comment is ignored.

Someone turns his or her back on me.

Someone leaves the room as soon as he or she sees me enter.

Yawning when listening to me.

Looking around the room rather than looking at me.

Not making the right listening noises (leaving out 'Mm. I see', 'Yes, of course').

Answering my questions in monosyllables (yes or no).

Going to the loo and never coming back.

Going to get a drink and never coming back.

Not smiling at me.

Not laughing at my jokes.

Not sharing in the conversation.

What feedback do you use with your parents?

(Do you sulk, are you grumpy with them, do you ignore them, do you answer as briefly as you can? Or do you smile and joke with them and show affection by touching and kissing?)

How do shy people behave?

They:

- avoid the person's eyes
- don't sound interested

- don't initiate conversation (introduce a subject to talk about)
- talk in monosyllables without expanding on anything
- don't make the right noises ('Mm', 'I see', 'Oh?') in the right places
- have a flat, quiet voice.

(These are similar to some of the ways described in negative feedback – so there is a risk that a shy person's behaviour is misinterpreted and people think she is not interested or is rude.)

Remember

You cannot expect positive feedback from others unless you use positive feedback yourself.

Task: Feedback Role-Plays

Act out the following scenes with the child, remembering about positive and negative feedback messages. Try to sustain the scenes for half a minute or so. If the child is very young you might like to do the role-play twice, the first time with you taking the child's place and the second time with the child using ideas from the way you acted in the same role.

Scene 1 (positive feedback)

You are an unexpected visitor (of the child's age) to the child's house. She has not seen you for over a year because you'd moved away. She is to greet you as warmly as possible and show interest in everything you have done up to now. She tells you how much she's missed you and wishes you lived closer. She is delighted when you tell her that your family's moving back for good.

SUGGESTIONS

'Hello! What are you doing here?'
'How lovely to see you! I've missed you so much!'

'You look well – and you've grown.'

'You're moving back? Great – but how come? I thought you weren't ever coming back.'

'Come in. Tell me everything. How long have you known? Why didn't you ring me?'

'Mum! Suzie's here. She's back for good!'

'Can I get you a drink? Something to eat?'

Scene 2 (negative feedback)

You are an unexpected visitor (of the child's age) to the child's house. Except this time, she is not pleased to see you and does not know how to handle your visit. She does not say outright for you to go away but neither is she welcoming.

SUGGESTIONS

'Oh.' (Stands across doorway making it obvious the person's not welcome to come in.)

'Really?' (In a bored tone.)

'I'm a bit busy right now. I've got lots of homework to do and then I've got to go out.'

'You're coming back? Are you pleased about that?' (You don't mention that you are.)

'How come?'

Scene 3 (positive feedback)

The child is a parent and you are his or her child. You have just passed your first music/gymnastics exam, for which you'd had to work extremely hard. Your parent is very pleased with you.

SUGGESTIONS

'I'm so proud of you. You deserved to do well after all the hard work you put in.'

'I know you didn't find it easy and that makes it all the more brilliant. You shall have a treat for tea and we'll think of something special to do at the weekend to celebrate.'

'How do you feel about it?'

'Let's 'phone grandma and tell her all the news. Then you can ring your friends.'

Scene 4 (negative feedback)

The child is a parent and you are his or her child. The parent has just found out that you took some money from her purse or wallet and used it to buy sweets.

SUGGESTIONS

Using an angry voice, arms folded and a finger pointing and wagging say:

'You've broken my trust.'

'You stole from me. I never thought a child of mine would ever steal from me.'

'You should be ashamed of yourself. How could you do it? I'm very disappointed in you.'

'How many other times have you done it? Do your friends steal?'

'You'd better watch it or you'll be had up for shoplifting next.'

'Who else knows about this?'

'What have you got to say for yourself?'

Task: Making Conversation

This task is about the child making conversation with someone of her own age whom she already knows well. (Making new friends was looked at in Chapter 3.) (It is too hard to expect a young child to chat to an adult and ensure that the conversation flows without any uncomfortable pauses – it is up to the adult to smooth over any difficulties in such circumstances.)

A child meeting a friend should look pleased to see him and interested in what he has to say, or he will consider her rude and poorly socially skilled. Discuss with the child the things she could talk about when meeting a friend, using the headings below as a framework, and write her suggestions down in her file.

What to talk about

- How the person is.
- How something went (such as a shopping trip or a football match).
- Anything important that's recently happened to me.
- How he's spent his time since he saw me last.
- How I've spent my time since I saw him last.
- Any trouble I've had – with other friends, parents or teachers.
- What we're going to do now.
- When we're next going to meet up.

How you would make sure the conversation is balanced

- Do not dominate (take over) the conversation. It is something that is shared between people.
- Once he has listened to my news, it is polite to ask him about his.
- Check his face when I talk to him to see whether he wants to interrupt me and, if it looks as though he does have something to say, pause to let him say it.

How would you check that you are not boring the person?

- By watching the expression on his face.
- By checking if he keeps eye contact with me: does he look around the room, looking for an escape route, or is he trying to be less bored?

- Is the person yawning or hanging on every word I say?
- Does the person say 'Yes, I see' or 'Really?' to show his interest or has he made no sounds of encouragement at all for the past five minutes?

What should you do if the person looks bored?

- Change the subject.
- Ask him about himself or something that I know he is interested in.
- Suggest we play a game or do something else.
- Invite the other person to choose what to do next.

Task: Role-Play: Making Conversation

Act out a scene with the child where she meets you, her best friend, in the park. The child should make sure she looks pleased to see you and is keen to chat. When she asks you about your day, make something up that a child of her age might have done. When she tells you about her day, she can actually describe it (unless she is older and more skilled, wanting to use her imagination).

Remind the child that she must check for feedback during the role-play – and act on it. Become bored. Does she notice and change the subject or pass the conversation back to you? When you look and sound extremely interested, does she give you more of the same or ignore your wish to know more and carry on regardless to a different topic?

After the role-play, ask the child how well she thought the conversation had gone. Had she noticed what you were particularly interested in? Had she noticed what had bored you? Tell her how you thought it went and between you, discuss what she could have done to improve the flow of conversation. (In real life, of course, this depends on both people co-operating and interpreting feedback.)

Conclusion

A child needs to:

- understand that she can communicate in many different ways with different people; some ways are inappropriate with some people, so must not be mixed up

- understand that good communication involves being open and clear about her needs and not expecting others to guess them

- be aware of her body language so that she can use it to reinforce her words – not to give a conflicting message

- watch out for feedback from others and adapt her behaviour when necessary

- be careful that she uses much positive feedback and reserves the negative feedback for only when it's necessary – otherwise she could make unnecessary difficulties for herself and make herself too many enemies

- watch other people's behaviour – their weaknesses and strengths – and learn from it

- practise talking to as many different people as possible; the more she makes conversation, the easier it becomes.

Chapter 14

The Art of Gifts and Compliments

This chapter is concerned with skilfully giving and receiving gifts and compliments: that is, in appropriate and rewarding ways to make both parties feel good about themselves. It is surprisingly difficult to do this with social grace. Hidden feelings and motives behind gifts and compliments might make it difficult for a person to accept them in a rewarding way. For example, if a child (or her parents) is rarely given a gift, she probably won't know how to respond. Or her parents might have told her she's not allowed to accept presents from people she doesn't know well – so the child might spend time puzzling out how well she knows the person rather than respond to accepting the gift.

As another example, if the child is not used to receiving compliments, she probably won't know how to give them or indeed be aware that they should be given. Or she might give them in a clumsy way that offends, rather than pleases, the person.

Giving and receiving gifts and compliments should always involve positive feedback so that the giver and receiver are rewarded by each other's behaviour.

Task: Receiving Gifts

Gifts should be received with grace. A person is doing a child a favour, or so they think, in giving the gift and they expect a positive response in return. It is rude to do otherwise. Discuss the following exercises with the child.

Exercise 1

You are given a book that you have already read as a birthday present from your aunt. What would you do and say?

(a) Say, 'Thank you. It's just what I wanted.'

(b) Say 'Thank you' and kiss her. You add that you've enjoyed other books by the same author.

(c) Tell her that you've already read the book and can't imagine wanting to read it a second time.

(d) Explain that although you've read it, you can use it to give to someone else as a present.

Option (a) is a lie and, unless you're good at acting, your aunt may see through it. Option (b) is not lying: you are only *implying* you haven't read the book. Your response would probably be interpreted as a compliment about her good taste in books as well as showing gratitude.

Option (c) is unkind and very rude and option (d) is insulting. Your aunt would not wish to think the only value you put on her present is that of saving you money when it comes to buying a present for a friend.

(You can sort out with your parents later about the possibility of changing the book. If they are present when the book is given to you and they keep quiet about you having read it, you must do the same. Take your lead from them.)

It is even better when you receive something that you genuinely like or are pleased with. But here, you need to be careful that you explain why the gift was a good choice to give the best thanks you can.

Exercise 2

Your uncle gives you a book on study skills. It is just what you wanted because you'd been having problems organising your work and revision for the end-of-year tests. What would be the best response?

(a) 'Thanks.'

(b) 'Oh, wow. This is just what I need. I've been having trouble with my studies.'

(c) 'Oh, I need something like this. Thanks.'

Options (a) and (c) are a bit flat: option (a) more than (c). Option (b) is much more rewarding to receive (very positive feedback).

Task: Receiving Gifts and Body Language

Discuss with the child how she should behave when she receives a gift. Would her behaviour depend on who had given her the gift and what it was? What should she *not* do when she receives a gift? Write down in the child's file a list of dos and don'ts that she needs to remember when receiving a gift. (Suggestions are given below.)

Expected and rewarding body language behaviour when receiving a gift

- Look very pleased: smile with my mouth and eyes.
- Hug and kiss the person.
- Hug the present to me (if I'm very young).
- Finger the present and show great interest in it.

Would your behaviour depend on the person who gave it to you?

- Yes. It would be inappropriate to hug someone I'd met only for the first time.
- I would be more physical with close relations than I would with anyone else.
- If I am a boy, I *might* be less physical with my friends because I am not used to close physical contact with them.
- If I am a girl, I *might* be more physical with my friends as I am used to hugging them.

Would your behaviour depend on what you had been given?

- Yes. I couldn't pretend I was over the moon about something that I didn't really want. It wouldn't be honest either.
- I would try to look as grateful as possible, even when I'm not too impressed with the gift.
- If I was delighted with something, I couldn't help showing it.

What should you not do when you receive a gift?

- Mumble 'Thanks'.
- Look at the floor or anywhere but in the person's eye when saying my thanks.
- Immediately put it down and get something more interesting to look at.
- Casually discard It (put it down) as though it were of no importance.
- Wrinkle my nose in dislike.
- Treat it so casually that I drop and break it.
- Sigh in disappointment.
- Say that I'd hoped it was going to be something else.
- Say that I've got hundreds of those already.

Task: Role-Plays: Receiving Gifts

Act out the following scenes with the child being the receiver of the present and you, the giver. Note the above questions when performing the role-plays and explain that you will be watching the child's body language as well as her verbal responses.

Role-play 1

Your father's best friend gives you a pair of jeans, wrapped in paper. When you undo the wrapping and see the jeans you love the look of them. The giver and your family are all in the room, waiting for your reaction.

SUGGESTIONS

Open the paper carefully. (It is only acceptable for the very young to rip open a present quickly. If an older person did this, people might think he or she was being greedy, so don't rush it.) Thank the giver very nicely and look pleased with the jeans (smile). Hold them against your body and look down to imagine what they would look like on.

You were not given the present by a close relative so it would be inappropriate to hug the person (unless your relationship with the person is special) but you could give a kiss.

A big compliment to the person would be immediately to go and try on the jeans and then parade around the room, showing them off to everyone.

DISCUSS

What would you do if, when you glanced at the label, you realised the jeans were too small for you? How would you feel? How would you hide these feelings?

SUGGESTIONS FOR DISCUSSION

Your happy feelings would probably turn into disappointment but you must not let this show. You could hide your disappointment by continuing to study the jeans until your face is back into a pleased expression and then become involved in thanking the person.

Sometimes, when people give gifts of clothes, they enclose the receipt in case it has to be changed or they ask, 'Did I get the size right?' If you are asked if the size is right, you could mention that you think they are too small, or sort it out with your parents later, after the giver has gone. (Even if the receipt is not enclosed, most shops will exchange items.)

Only suggest trying the jeans on if invited to (as you know they won't fit properly) – however, if you are invited to, all should become clear without you having to say anything when you can't do up the zip!

Role-play 2

Your great aunt gives you a box of toffees. She had won them at Bingo and is very glad to be able to give them to you even though she likes them herself. However, you hate toffees and wished she had kept them for herself. Your family is in the same room as you, waiting for your reaction.

SUGGESTIONS

You must thank your great aunt very nicely – remember that she has made a sacrifice for you. She gave you something she'd have enjoyed eating herself. She would definitely expect a kiss and possibly a hug too, depending on how well you know her

You must look delighted with the toffees. Nothing less will give your great aunt the pleasure she deserves. Less than this would seem ungracious and everyone would feel annoyed with you. (But don't overdo it and say that toffees are your favourite sweets – or you'll probably be given a few more boxes of them over the next few years.)

You could open the box and offer them around (to get them eaten) – but if you do that, you must have one yourself. If you cannot bear toffees, then don't open the box in the giver's presence.

Task: How to React When the Gift is for Someone Else

It is hard for a child to hide disappointment and jealousy but it is a valuable skill to learn. Adults who can successfully do this avoid loss of face, which is very important to them. (For example, if a colleague gets the promotion you yourself had sought, you would hide your own feelings and pretend that you were pleased for him – with no 'hard feelings'.)

Discuss the given situation with the child.

Imagine that something you always wanted was given to your older brother by your uncle. You are in the room at the time. How would you feel? How should you act or behave? What should you say? What shouldn't you do?

SUGGESTIONS

How would you feel?	Very jealous. Angry that he's got something I want. Eaten up inside. Disbelieving.
How should you act or behave?	I should try to pretend I'm glad for my older brother even though I'm eaten up with jealousy. Later, I could confide in my brother or my parents that I feel bad because he got something I'd really wanted.
What should you say?	'Aren't you lucky!' 'That's perfect.' 'You must be so pleased.' Admit to always wanting one, as long as it doesn't come out like a moan or a whine, wishing it had been given to me.
What shouldn't you do?	I should not walk out of the room as soon as the gift is given. I should not show any signs of jealousy in front of the giver – it would embarrass him and make him feel uncomfortable. I should not try to destroy the thing out of jealousy, believing that if I can't have one, my brother can't have his. I should not be deliberately mean to my brother – he had not been given a present deliberately to make me jealous.

Task: Giving Gifts

Giving a gift loses its meaning if it is done with bad grace or in a socially clumsy way: this takes much of the pleasure out of receiving it. A child needs to learn how to bestow a gift graciously so that the receiver is complimented as much by the giving as the gift itself.

Discuss the following exercises with the child.

Exercise 1

You have just had a row with your mum. However, it is her birthday and you still haven't given her the present you'd bought her. You don't feel like giving it to her now because you think she's been unfair to you but you know it must be done. How do you give the present?

(a) You chuck it on the table in front of your mum and then walk out of the room again, without saying a word.

(b) You tell your mum that although you don't feel she deserves her present, she may as well have it as you've spent your money on it.

(c) You go to your room to cool off for a while and then go back to your mum and say 'Happy birthday' and hand her the present.

(d) You leave the present by your mum's bed so that she finds it that night – after you've gone to bed.

(e) You go straight up to your mum and hug and kiss her and wish her happy birthday.

Options (a), (b) and (d) are not gracious ways of giving a present. It would give your mum no pleasure to get your present when it has been given to her with so little ceremony. Option (e) may be unlikely since you have not yet cleared the air over the row you've had. Option (c) would probably be the most appropriate. It would then be up to your mum to help smooth things over and combine making up with thanking you for your present.

Exercise 2

Your friend is emigrating to Brussels and you want to say goodbye to her and give her a gift that you have especially made for her. You arrive at her house, ten minutes before her family leaves, for the final goodbye and you give her the present that you've brought with you. How do you do this?

(a) Say, 'This is for you. Goodbye.'

(b) Say, 'I've made this for you as a goodbye present. I'm going to miss you and hope I'll see you again sometime.'

(c) Push the present through her letterbox and run away.

(d) Give the present to her mum and ask her to pass it on to your friend.

Option (b) is by far the best. You have taken the time to explain why you are there and that you made the present yourself and what it's for. You have also told your friend that you valued her friendship because you are going to miss her. Option (a) is the next best because you are giving the present to her in person and you have spoken to her. The other options are not appropriate. You need to give your friend an opportunity to say thank you and to say goodbye properly.

Task: Giving Gifts and Body Language

Discuss with the child how she should behave when she gives a gift, using the following headings as a framework. Then write down in the child's file appropriate and inappropriate 'giving' behaviour that she needs to remember.

What would be expected and rewarding body language behaviour?

• Stand and face the person.

• Make eye contact.

- Stand quite close. No one would expect me to stand halfway across the room when I give a gift.

- Smile as I give the gift.

- Tell the person what it is for (his birthday or a 'thank you' for all the help he'd given me).

- Wait to see his reaction.

- Be prepared to receive his thanks and to say, 'That's all right.'

- If the gift needs explanation, give it (for example, if it's in parts, how it fits together).

NOTE

The gift should be wrapped in appropriate paper. For example, if it's someone's birthday, you shouldn't give the present wrapped up in wedding or Christmas paper. You could wrap it in paper you've decorated yourself.

Would your behaviour depend on whom the gift is for?

- If the gift were for a close relative, I could expect to be hugged in thanks – and I could hug and kiss the person when I give the present.

- If the gift were for someone less close, for example my teacher, I would not expect to hug or kiss either in giving, or in receiving, thanks.

What should you not do when you give a gift?

- Giggle.

- Look away from the person.

- Mumble or say nothing.

- Give the gift without saying anything.

- Put the gift down in front of the person and then walk out without waiting for the person to open the present or to even acknowledge it. (I should hand the gift to the person and wait for a response.)

- Walk out before the person has a chance to open the present. (It is usual in Western culture to watch as the present is opened, unlike in China where the present is opened in private. However, if it's an early Christmas or birthday present, the person may prefer to unwrap the present on the actual day.)

- Accept the person's thanks ungraciously. (I could say, 'I'm glad you like it – I wasn't sure whether it was the right thing.')

Task: Role-Plays: Giving Gifts

Act the following scenes with the child being the giver of the present and you, the receiver. Consider the above questions when performing the role-plays and explain that you will be watching the child's body language as well as her verbal responses.

Role-play 1

You have a box of chocolates to give to your teacher at the end of the summer term. Next year you'll be in a different class and will have a different teacher, so it's your way of saying thank you for what she's done and goodbye.

SUGGESTION

Go to the teacher at the end of your last lesson with her and hand her the present saying, 'This is for you. I want to say thank you for all you've done for me and I'll miss you next year.'

Keep eye contact and smile as you pass her the present. Wait for anything she has to say ('It's been a pleasure having you in my class') and then reply to it, if appropriate ('Thank you').

Role-play 2

You give your mum her Christmas (or other celebratory) present.

SUGGESTION

Say 'Happy Christmas, Mum', giving her a hug and a kiss as you give the present. You wait for her to open it and readily receive her kiss and hug in return. You explain to her why you got it ('I know your favourite group/author/chocolates…so I thought you'd like this/these'). Watch her as she examines the present and reads any blurb on the packaging. Take time to be with her while she absorbs what it is she's been given so that you can receive all the nice comments she has to give. ('Oh, it's just what I wanted. How kind of you. Thank you so much.')

Task: Receiving Compliments

When a person pays a child a compliment, he or she is doing it to be nice to her and expects her to be pleased to receive it. If she doesn't respond to the compliment as hoped, the person who gave it may feel silly and regret having said it in the first place. This is unlikely to make him or her want to compliment the child again.

Exercise 1

Grandma sees you in a pair of trousers for the first time and says, 'That's a nice pair of trousers.' But you are wearing old clothes that you hate. Do you:

(a)   Tell Grandma that you hate the clothes and why.

(b)   Say, 'No it's not.'

(c)   Say, 'Thank you.'

If you are very close to your Grandma and can explain why you hate the clothes, option (a) might be acceptable (for example, if your elder brother or sister used to wear them and you'd wanted to be able to choose your own clothes). However, if you hate them for a reason that is obvious and visible (such as patches, fades or holes), Grandma might think you were criticising her for not noticing the worn state they are in.

With option (b), you are completely throwing the compliment back at Grandma like an unwanted present. This is both rude and unkind.

Option (c) is the best response. If Grandma should later notice that the clothes you are wearing are old and faded, so be it. It is tactful of you not to point it out.

Exercise 2

If your uncle tells you that you have a great singing voice but you know there are others in your class who are better, what do you say?

(a) 'Thank you.'

(b) 'No, I can't sing.'

(c) 'There are loads in my class with a better voice.'

The best option is (a). It is a simple, straightforward response – your uncle has complimented you and you are thanking him for that. (You don't have to agree with him.) Option (c) is the next acceptable, although rather ungracious and it unnecessarily puts yourself down. However, it does give your uncle the chance to rescue the compliment and say, 'Well, I've not heard the others sing but I have heard you and I still think your voice is great.'

Option (b) is the worst response, totally rejecting your uncle's opinion and telling him he has no ear for music.

Task: Giving Compliments

Sometimes, compliments sound stilted or false. Whenever a child gives a compliment, it should include something that she genuinely means. If it is not genuine she will probably be found out and then her words will not be trusted. She must also look and sound as though she means what she says or her words will count for nothing.

Discuss the following examples with the child.

Example 1

Saying that someone's had a nice hair cut in a flat voice sounds as though you are just going through the motion of complimenting because you think that's what's expected of you.

SUGGESTION

- Distinguish differences. ('The ends are really neat now. Many were split before.')

- Notice and remark on the out of the ordinary: not on everyday things. ('You've had highlights put in.')

- Compare how the hair was with how it is now (as long as you've got something positive to say). ('That shorter style really suits you.')

Example 2

If you tell someone how nice she looks every time you see her, she will know that you say it no matter what she looks like. So when she does look special (such as when going to a party), she will count your compliment as worthless.

This does not mean that you should hardly ever give compliments. However, it does mean that you must make them meaningful to the person you are giving them to – and you cannot do that if you compliment someone on what he or she is wearing every time you see them.

If you never dish out compliments, people will think that you are mean or that you don't bother to notice anything. You need to find a balance.

Can you think of times when you could give meaningful compliments?

Think back over the past few days when you have been with people, gone to their houses or have just met them after a break. What could you have said or done to compliment? The more you practise giving imaginary compliments, the easier you will be able to identify opportunities and think of positive and genuine things to say.

SUGGESTIONS

- When I leave a friend's house I should tell him and his parents what a great time I had.
- When one of my parents has cooked my favourite meal, or when I particularly enjoy a meal, I should compliment the person who cooked it.
- When I'm bought a gift I should say it's what I wanted or why I like it.
- When I'm given a treat I should say how much I enjoyed it.
- When my friend has something new that I like I should tell him what I think of it.
- When a friend does something well or has learnt a new skill, such as his first handstand or cartwheel, I should praise him. (It doesn't matter if I can do it better: I can still praise his progress.)
- Laughing when someone says something funny is a compliment using body language. (I can also say, 'That was really funny.')
- Smiling when I see someone is also a compliment using body language. (I can also enthusiastically say 'Hello' or 'Hi' to show I am pleased to see him or her.)

Task: Non-Compliments

Non-compliments are when a child says something that doesn't hit the mark and actually refers to something else. These are not compliments at all and can make the receiver feel very uncomfortable. Non-compliments are a form of put-down and should be avoided at all costs, unless the aim is to offend.

Use the following examples to explain to the child what non-compliments are.

Example 1

You are celebrating passing a difficult exam. Someone says to you, 'I don't know what the fuss is about. You knew you'd pass.'

This does not compliment you at all – your success has been taken for granted. The other person did not feel it was worth while to praise you, which was very ungenerous. Even if you were expected to pass, you still deserve recognition of the fact that you have achieved something. It does not make it less worth while.

Example 2

You score a goal in football. Everyone in your team crowds round you and cheers, except one who says, 'You'd have had to be a moron to miss from that position.'

This is very ungenerous and implies that anyone could have scored the goal. You deserve to be praised for it – you might have slipped and delivered the kick into the goalie's arms or been tackled at the last moment. You did something praiseworthy and that ought to be recognised.

Discussion

Now discuss with the child why people give non-compliments.

(Often people are very stingy with their compliments because they are not generous-hearted and hate to see others do well. Usually, a non-compliment arises from jealousy or a feeling of superiority – the person thinks he or she is better than the other. Another reason is that someone has poor social skills and doesn't know any better.)

Exercise

Ask the child to think of non-compliments she has been given. (These should then be written down in her file.) What could she say to each person who gave her a non-compliment? (This can then be written down too.) Her response must be assertive: it must not insult the person or call the person names.

Non-compliments may need to be collected over a period of time as the child may not be able to recall any immediately. She might also not remember any because she didn't recognise them as non-compliments at the time. She might have felt disappointed with what the person had said, but was not sure why.

If she can't think of any she has been given, she could try to think of assertive responses to the two examples given above. However, she should keep on the watch for non-compliments given to her – or anyone else – and note them down. They are useful to collect as they will give her a good insight to the minds of others and reveal others' weaknesses and jealousies. They also give the child the opportunity to work out responses for them so that, should she come across them again, she will be prepared and can protect herself or a friend.

EXAMPLES

Non-compliment 1: You are celebrating passing a difficult exam. Someone says to you, 'I don't know what the fuss is about. You knew you'd pass.'

> *Response 1: 'If I knew I'd pass I wouldn't have been so worried.*
> *However, I did pass and have the right to celebrate the occasion.'*

Non-compliment 2: You score a goal in football. Everyone in your team crowds round you and cheers, except one who says, 'You'd have had to be a moron to miss from that position.'

> *Response 2: 'Aren't you pleased I scored a goal for your side?'*
>
> *Or: 'Are you jealous it was I who scored and not you?'*
>
> *Or: 'I'm obviously not a moron then.'*

Task: Finding Something to Say When You Can't Compliment

This is probably the hardest way of complimenting – when the child is desperately searching for something to say and just cannot see anything positive to comment on, yet someone certainly expects her to say something. However, it mustn't be a lie or the person will see through it. (This section is similar to 'Task: Tact in Bypassing the Awful', in Chapter 11.)

Do the following exercises with the child.

Exercise 1

You are given a meal which is completely new to you by a friend's parent and you can only just bear to eat it. When asked if you like it, what should you say?

(a) 'No, it's horrible.'

(b) 'I'm not sure. I haven't had anything like this before and it's strange to me. It's certainly interesting.'

(c) 'Mm. It's lovely, thanks.'

If you use option (a) you will definitely offend. If you use the last, you risk getting that meal every time you go to your friend's house. Option (b) may not be very complimentary but it is truthful – albeit not the whole truth. Also, this response may invite a get-out from the parent: 'Well, if you decide you don't like it please don't force yourself to eat it.'

Exercise 2

Try to think of positive responses you could make in the following circumstances (or carefully avoid answering the question).

1. You are invited to see a pantomime with a friend and his family. You thought it completely silly and did not appreciate the racist and sexist jokes (making fun of people from other ethnic groups and putting girls down). At the end, your

friend's parents ask you what you thought of it. What would you say?

Response: 'The set and the costumes were fantastic. They must have put loads of work into it. I thought the bit where…was very funny. Thank you for bringing me to see it.'

(Ignore all your personal criticism.)

2. Your friend fancies a girl whom he points out to you on the way home from school. He asks you what you think of her – but you don't think much of her.

   Response: 'How can I say when I don't know her and I only got a glimpse of her? What do you like about her?'

3. A friend shows you a game she got for her birthday that you already have. You hate the game. She's expecting you to be impressed that she's got it too now.

   Response: 'It's ages since I played this. Would you like a game?'

   Or: 'It is a really good game.' (If she asks you to play it with her you can't refuse without making her feel bad.)

Conclusion

A child needs to concentrate on being polite and kind when giving and receiving gifts and compliments, giving the person the attention he or she deserves and not rushing through the procedures. She must also remember that it is up to her to be sensitive to the other person's feelings and, as far as possible, say something rewarding.

A child needs to be able to recognise non-compliments as a form of put-down and protect herself from them. She must also be careful that she does not use them herself. If a compliment is intended, it should be sufficiently generous to leave no doubt in the receiver's mind that it is a genuine compliment.

Chapter 15

Helping and Caring Skills

Throughout life, a child will need help and emotional support from others. She will also often be in a position where she needs to offer help and care in return. None of us can live life in a sterile environment where we exist without interacting with others and without, at times, needing their support.

Children are unlikely to be skilful at giving such help. It is a sign of maturity to be able to offer emotional support to others, and children frequently clumsily fumble with other people's feelings before they get the hang of it. (For children, this is made more difficult because they will be meeting each situation for the very first time. By the time we are adults, we have experienced many repeats of situations, learning through our mistakes and successes how best to handle a person's distress – although we still do come across new situations. But here again, we have the advantage of having had more life experience so are more likely to judge our sympathetic responses better.)

Because vulnerable feelings are at stake, it is very important for the sake of the child's friendships to understand what is required of her. Too often, children are completely at a loss as to how to handle a situation. They need much help and support from a caring adult in order to do this.

Task: Role-Plays: Listening Skills

In order to show sympathy and understanding, a child needs to show the right body language when she is listening to someone's troubles. Pretend you are the child's friend and you have problems you want to tell her about. She must listen sympathetically and be as helpful as possible to you when you have difficulty telling your problems. Note the body language the child uses and discuss it with her after the role-play.

You could do several role-plays and swap roles so that the child learns how to look when someone is listening sympathetically. Make a list of positive listening body language in the child's file, discussing each aspect with her (suggestions are given later).

Below is a suggested list of problems. Some of these are unsuitable for younger children and have been included for the older child who needs to be aware of some of the more challenging problems people face. However, even if the problem is suited to the child's age, you must be comfortable about bringing up the issues with the child. Once you have chosen a problem, use your imagination to embellish it.

Please note that this task is linked to the one following: 'Task: Role-Play: Reporting Back'.

Suggested problems

- You are about to start a new class with a new teacher and are worried about it.
- You have fallen out with your best friend.
- Your pet hamster died.
- You think the teachers don't like you.
- Your homework got dropped in a puddle and you don't think the teachers will believe that it wasn't your fault.
- You are terrified of spiders.
- You are upset because your face is so spotty.
- You feel no one takes you seriously.
- You don't believe in God any more.
- You've got a bad school report and are frightened about what your parents will do and say.
- You are being bullied.
- Your parents are out of work and there's not enough money for food and clothes.
- You are frightened of travelling on buses and this is a problem since you travel to school on one.
- A teacher has been picking on you.

- You are going out with a boy/girl for the first time and don't know what to expect.
- You are upset because your friends have much more freedom than you.
- Your parents are divorcing.
- Your parents argue a great deal.
- Your older sister has run away and no one knows where she has gone.
- You don't like your body size.
- You live in a children's home and wish you were with a caring family.
- Your mother is an alcoholic.
- You think you might be pregnant.
- Your best friend has an imaginary boyfriend and you don't know whether to challenge her about it or let her continue making up stories of where they go together and what they do.
- You think you are homosexual but daren't tell your family.
- You feel that your life is too restricted by your family's traditional values.
- You want to become a vegetarian but your parents don't take it seriously.
- You want to have your eyebrow and tongue pierced but your parents won't let you. (You are under age.)
- You're not happy but don't know why.

Listening body language

- Make eye contact.
- Face the person.
- Look serious.
- Look interested.
- Try not to look shocked if you hear anything surprising (the person might lose confidence in you).

- Feel and express outrage if an injustice has been done to your friend.
- Lean towards the person.
- Make appropriate listening noises. ('Mm. I see.')

As well as listening appropriately, when the child is in the role of the troubled person, she needs to tell her problems in an appropriate manner. For example, she will not be taken seriously if she giggles while telling her problems.

Task: Role-Play: Reporting Back

As well as making the right body actions and the right verbal sounds when listening to a friend in trouble, a child also needs to pay attention to the content of what is said. Use the problems you have just acted out for this role-play.

The child has just listened to her friend's problems. Now she must relate them to a third person because her friend is too upset to do this herself. (This is good practice for being a 'witness' – relating things to a teacher or parent or the police.) It is important for the child not to repeat everything that was said to her. She must sum up the difficulties and tell them in as concise a way as she can. (Although if she were a witness for the police, they would probably want every detail.)

Things to check
Did the child:

- fully understand the situation?
- explain in as concise a way as possible?
- stick to facts? (For example, her opinion was not asked for: her friend might be hurt if she said something to belittle her problem.)
- repeat the problem accurately?

Task: Helping a Friend in Trouble

Ask the child to think about the things that she needs when she is in trouble of any kind and use these to make a list in her file concerning what to do when a friend needs help.

What to do when a friend needs help

SUGGESTIONS

- Give all my attention to my friend.
- Listen carefully.
- Check I understand what he's saying by repeating back what he's said. ('Are you saying that...')
- Give him a hug or touch his arm.
- Be sympathetic.
- Give support by suggesting what he could do or by being with him and asking every so often how he is.
- Be understanding.
- Be kind.
- Understand that many problems are ongoing: they don't just disappear overnight. Expect to keep hearing about my friend's difficulties.
- Be prepared to hear things I've heard before. People in distress often keep going over the same ground and repeating themselves.
- Be prepared to encourage him to seek adult help if I think he ought to or if I am out of my depth.

Rules for listening to troubles

When you listen to your friend's troubles there are certain unwritten rules you should follow. What do you think they might be?

SUGGESTIONS

- Don't repeat the conversation without my friend's permission.
- Don't gossip about my friend.
- If I suspect he's so upset he might harm himself or I know he's not adequately looking after himself, I should tell an adult I trust. (This could be a teacher, one of my parents or my friend's parents or a relative.)
- If I am upset about the things I have been told and they are troubling me, I must tell an adult I can trust so that I talk it over with someone sensible who can help me.
- If I think I am out of my depth with my friend's problems, ask him to tell an adult or to ring Childline on 0800 1111 – or do it for him.
- If he believes he has a problem, I should accept that he has. I mustn't belittle it, or him, for being troubled over it.

Task: Extension Role-Play: Basic Counselling Skills

This task is more appropriate for teenagers, since a higher level of understanding and a greater level of skill are required to carry it out. Also, the role-play suggestions are inappropriate for a younger child to handle.

First discuss the following rules with the child and check that she understands what they mean.

Basic counselling rules

- You must show respect for the person who confides in you.
- You must not show that you are shocked by what is said.
- You must not judge.
- You must be sympathetic.

- You must be empathetic (put yourself in the other person's shoes to imagine what he or she is going through).

- You must not tell the person what to do. You may only give suggestions. ('Have you thought about…?' or, 'Have you tried…?')

- Ask the person how he felt at the time or how he feels now. Don't be afraid to discuss feelings.

- If appropriate, discuss with the person how he could move on from his problems or come to terms with them.

- Know when to pass the problem on to a professional or someone more experienced than you, such as a parent, teacher or other trusted adult.

Now think up a challenging problem (or choose one of the more challenging problems listed earlier or one from the list below) and see how the older child deals with supporting you and handles what is said. Young adults tend to be very judgemental and see things as definitely right or wrong, yet life is not like that. The idea of this role-play is to challenge the child's view of life while giving her an emotionally difficult situation to counsel.

If, for whatever reason, you do not wish to use one of the suggested problems, think up one of your own. However, bear in mind that it is meant to challenge the child and test whether she can succeed in being non-judgemental and objective: she must not give her point of view or dollop out advice or make you feel bad about what you are telling her.

Suggested problems

- You (or your girlfriend) have had a pregnancy terminated and you feel grief, guilt and remorse.

- You have stolen from shops and don't seem able to stop doing it.

- You feel suicidal and it frightens you.

- You have an eating disorder that has got out of control and is taking over your life.

- You have had underage sex and you are scared someone will find out.

- You are homosexual and don't know what to do about it.

- A close family friend keeps touching you in a way that makes you feel uncomfortable.

- You have tried Ecstasy and want to take it again but you know it's madness to risk your life.

- You cannot leave your room until it is perfectly tidy. You worry about it being messed up when you are in school and can't concentrate in lessons. (You have an Obsessive Compulsive Disorder.)

- You have been raped when out on a date but are too afraid to tell your parents because you think they will blame you.

Post role-play discussion

- Ask the child how she felt, hearing the things she did. How hard was it to be non-judgemental?

- Why should she not give advice? (So that she is not blamed if the advice is followed and things go wrong. Also, so that the person finds his own solution by discussing options with a caring person. Taking responsibility for helping himself helps him to feel proud that he has coped and boosts his self-esteem.)

- Ask the child what she should do if someone confides in her about a problem that she has fixed views on. (For example, if someone confides she has had an abortion and the child cannot accept that there are any acceptable grounds for having one. In such a case, she should stop the person divulging everything and say she is not the best person to talk to about it. Then she should suggest someone else the person could go to.)

Task: When to Say 'No' to Problems

There will be times when a child has too many problems of her own, is out of her depth or cannot look sympathetically on something the person has done, and will therefore not be able to give non-judgemental help. In such circumstances, the child must draw a boundary and prevent the person from crossing it with all his problems.

What things could you say to deflect someone's problems?

In other words, what could you say to show the person that, although you are sympathetic, you are not the right person to be listening to his problems now? Try to think up sentences for a few different situations.

SUGGESTIONS

- 'I'm sorry, I don't know anything about that sort of thing. Is there an adult you trust whom you could go to?' (You could then suggest one of the following: an aunt or uncle; a teacher; his doctor; an older brother or sister; or his parents.)

- 'I'm very sorry but I've so many problems myself that I can't deal with another at the moment. Have you thought about talking to…? It's not that I don't care, it's just that right now I'm not the best person to ask.'

- 'I found Mr X really helpful when I had a similar problem – he'd be the best person to see. Then we could talk about what he said.'

- 'I'm busy now – if I don't finish this work, Ms Maharaj may chuck me out of the class like she threatened. Could you come back at 4 pm? I should be finished by then and will give you my undivided attention.'

- 'I think you must see a doctor. I can't give you any advice over this, it wouldn't be safe.'

- 'I don't know what you should do but our teacher might. Would you like me to come with you?'

- 'I haven't a clue about what you should do. I think this problem's too big for either of us. You need to speak to an adult about it.'

It is important that the child knows she does not have to have all the right answers and that it is OK to suggest finding help elsewhere. This is not abandoning a friend's problems but helping her find someone who can help appropriately.

Parental Pages on Helping and Caring Skills

Photocopiable for professional use within the institution that bought the book, to use to aid parents develop their child's helping and caring skills.

Dealing with a friend's bereavement

It is important to give your child ideas on how to help a bereaved friend when the situation occurs, since she will most likely be out of her depth. This will help her friend, giving her an emotional 'crutch': she will know she can talk to your child whenever she needs help.

You will also help your child become more socially skilled, developing her emotional depth and understanding. (She doesn't just think of her friend, poor thing, but really tries to understand what it must be like for her friend to lose someone close.)

Helping your child through such an emotional learning experience encourages her to open up to you about her friend and on other occasions when she does not know how to handle the situation. She will see you as an emotional support for herself and will understand the importance of discussing emotional problems with you and others.

Task: Exercise for Parents

This task is for parents to discuss with the professional in the child's absence. The information is to be at hand for the parent in case it is needed.

No role-play has been suggested because it may cause unnecessary stress to your child: she may not find herself in such a position until she is in her late teens or so. It may also cause unnecessary stress to your child through brooding about a close bereavement happening to her. It is better to be ready to deal with the situation as it arises than prepare your child for a tragic and distressing event that might not happen.

Imagine your child has just been called up by a friend, Harry, to say his father's died and could he go round? What advice would you give to your child? (Try to think up your own ideas before reading the given suggestions.)

SUGGESTIONS

- Go round straight away (after being given advice).
- Be gentle.
- Say how sorry you are.
- Ask him what happened.
- Give physical comfort, but be sensitive to him not wanting it. (It might be hard for some boys to give each other physical comfort because of 'Western' social expectations. However, boys still need to be comforted. Try not to fear the rejection but give it a go anyway. Don't feel hurt if you are rejected: it doesn't mean that your friendship and kind thoughts are rejected too.)
- Be prepared for him to cry, and offer a shoulder to cry on. (If he cries, he is more likely to accept a hug.)
- Stay with him for as long as you can and for as long as you feel welcome.
- Reassure him and say when you'll be round to see him again.
- Ask about the family's plans: when is the funeral going to be? Is he going to have time off school until after the funeral? Perhaps these things haven't been thought of yet.
- Let the conversation drift, allowing your friend to take the lead.
- Silences are OK. Try not to feel embarrassed about them.
- Offer to tell people about his dad for him and to get work from school if he wants it (or anything else you think he would want).
- Ask what you could do to help.

- Be prepared to do some of the things you usually do when you're round at his house, such as play music and discuss bands or play board games. It might be important to your friend to continue doing some of the 'normal' things.

If your child has already experienced some form of bereavement (animal or human) you could remind her of the feelings she had at the time so that she could imagine what Harry is feeling now. It might help her be sympathetic towards him.

Conclusion

Helping people is a tricky and imprecise area in which to work. There are often no hard and fast rules. Much depends on whom you are dealing with and what has happened. However, there is always the need to be sympathetic and under-standing, even when a child cannot understand why someone is so upset. If the person perceives he has a problem then the child must accept that and consider ways to help him, regardless of whether she considers him to have a 'real' problem.

However, this does not mean that the child should burden herself with every-one's problems. It is perfectly acceptable to point the person gently in another direction, explaining why someone else is in a better position to help him this time. As the child gets older and gains experience, she will become more confident about giving help. However, the child must always remember to be very careful in what she says and how she says it. People in need are extremely vulnerable and the situation can easily be made worse with a few incautious words. Visualising what comments might help her if she were in that situation might avoid this pitfall.

Helping and listening skills are useful throughout life, for developing rela-tionships in and out of work. Learning to become a caring and responsible adult is an integral part of growing up and reaps the rewards of being trusted and respected in the community within which the child interacts.

Summary

This book has shown the child:

- who she is and how she views herself
- how to see herself in a more positive light and boost her self-esteem
- how to recognise her strengths and weaknesses and how to improve them
- the difference between positive and negative behaviour and the rewards and penalties to expect for each
- how to consider family rules and expectations and understand why certain behaviour brings certain penalties
- that all areas of society have rules in order to ensure expected behaviour in certain places and at certain times and within certain situations
- how to observe warning signs and modify her behaviour as a result to avoid trouble
- how to make friends and keep them
- that people behave differently with different people and in different environments
- how to read body language and produce her own body language to reflect what she is saying and how she feels
- how to be assertive and stand up for herself
- how to show feelings in an appropriate way and control negative feelings
- how to keep herself safe
- how to communicate to achieve a greater understanding between people
- how to make conversation
- how to combat shyness
- how to give gifts and compliments gracefully
- how to receive gifts and compliments in a positive way
- how to show care and help those in trouble
- to recognise there are some things with which she cannot help.

Parental Pages: Suggestions to Reinforce the Course

Photocopiable for professional use within the institution that bought the book, to use to help parents incorporate this course into the child's everyday life.

1. Whenever your child anticipates a social occasion or when she needs to communicate with someone else, it is possible for her to do a role-play beforehand with you, to remind her what to do and what not to do and to give her confidence about doing it.

2. If there is not the time for a quick role-play or neither of you have the inclination, give a quick reminder to your child of what you expect. ('Always look the person in the eyes when you say "Hello" or "Goodbye". Smile and look as though you are pleased to see him. Don't forget to say "Thank you" if you are passed anything at the table.')

3. When an opportunity arises for your child to interact with someone, she can be given a 'social skills challenge'. (An example would be to return something that you had borrowed from a friend and to relay a simple thanks message.) Let her look upon it as some sort of game where she must try to remember what she has been shown in this course and put it into practice. After her challenge, you could both discuss the good and bad points. What would she do another time?

4. After a social occasion with the child (you may have been to lunch at someone's house), discuss any social mistakes you observed in others or yourselves. What should the person, or you, have done or said – or not done or said? If you take the trouble to observe, there is a great deal you can learn just by watching other people.

5. After a social occasion with others, discuss any skilful handling of a tricky situation that you observed. Can you or your child think of a better way or an equally acceptable alternative?

It cannot be emphasised enough that children need constant reminding of expectations and good social practices. If your child makes a social blunder that you know you ought to have warned against, do not blame her as it is important not to dishearten her with failure.

In these ways, this course is continued so that it becomes a part of your child's life. It will also make you more aware of how to help your child – and perhaps yourself. It is a rare person indeed who makes no social mistakes, ever.